THE TWELVE STORIES OF

Christmas

BY REV. S LINDY PURDY

D1709824

ACKNOWLEDGMENTS

It took twelve years and a community of folks to get this book into print. I was inspired to write my first story for the Women's Christmas Tea in 2004. Some early encouragers, Stephanie Hennings, Jim Zimmerman, Bill Boulware and others, thought they might be publishable. So now, twelve stories later, I am so pleased to share them with you.

Thanks also to the artists who imaginatively drew, painted and photographed the illustrations for this book. They include Jim Turner, my artistic brother, his son Mitchell, my dear friend Marla, local art instructor Brian Doeden, and Marnie Baehr and Camilla Farley.

I am forever grateful to the community to Wayzata Community Church, for they have been the inspiration for this special time in my life and my desire to write.

I dedicate this book to my mother "Meme" who attended every Christmas Tea with joy and encouragement. Her favorite story was "The Angel Harold." Notice the exquisite watercolor that illustrates this story, done by her son, Jim.

Special thanks to Camilla Farley and Marnie Baehr for their editorial savvy, creativity and hard work; production of this book is only possible because of their efforts.

These stories are meant to be read aloud, so find a comfy chair, sip on a cup of tea and enjoy a story or two.

Merry Christmas,
Lindy Purdy

ISBN: 978-1-4951-8242-6
Printed in the United States of America.

FORWARD

Christmas traditions are the fabric of most families, many organizations and certainly faith communities. For the past twelve years, I have been honored to serve the women of Wayzata Community Church by serving tea and coffee at the annual Women's Christmas Tea. Fellowship, beautiful tables and delectable desserts abound. All in attendance are treated to an original story of the season that is thoughtful, joyful, funny and truly inspiring. Each year Lindy's story has been important in setting the stage for the season.

Lindy has a unique gift of weaving a great message into a story that is memorable and full of characters that will bring to life either someone from your past or one that you wish you could call your friend. So, enjoy twelve years of amazing creativity, fun and the true meaning of Christmas. I wish I could be at your Christmas celebration to witness the joy of your family and friends when you read Lindy's words.

May your Holidays be blessed by these stories of love, life and the magic that only happens at Christmas.

Bill Boulware
Wayzata Community Church Staff

Contents

The Year I Got to Play Mary in the Christmas Pageant

by S. Lindy Purdy

I knew all the lines. They were etched in my brain. I had said them over and over and over again—to my mom, to Grandpa, to my big brother in those rare moments when he would listen, and even to my little sister when I bribed her with M&M's. The words were as clear as a bell and I had all the inflections just right.

You see, in my church, the Christmas pageant is the highlight of the year. Scripts are handed out on the second Sunday in September, and auditions are held the week before Halloween. When everyone else in the neighborhood was deciding what to be for Trick-or-Treat, the kids from Perfect Savior United Church of Christ were waiting impatiently to learn what costume they would wear on December 24th.

Up until this year, I had always been content to be part of the multitude. I was a sheep for a couple years, one of the ones you could find crouching in the back of the stage, too frightened even to say our one line—"baaaa." When I was too old for that, I was one of the cluster of angels moving onto the stage like an amoeba, shouting "Gloria" in perfect unison, then moving into the wings. Only, I never actually made a sound—for fear of being heard. Then for the last two years I was one of the townspeople. They don't say anything; they just loiter, or is that linger?

Everyone agreed that my roles had suited me well. In my everyday life, I was the one who sat in the back of the classroom and never spoke. I was the one who always had the weekly Bible verse memorized, but never raised my hand to recite it. I was good at blending in with the other sheep and angels and townspeople—not just on December 24th, but all year long.

You should have seen the look on my mom's face at the dinner table on the second Sunday in September, the day we got the script in Sunday School. I proudly announced I was going to try out for the part of Mary. There was an awkward silence. Grandpa recovered first. "Gosh, that's wonderful, Jenny." He had that fake smile on his face. Then my mom joined in, "If that's what you'd like to do, that's wonderful. But you were so good as a townsperson last year. Wouldn't you like to do that again this year?" Even my big brother, Larry, known for his snide comments, had a worried look on his face. "Gee, Jen, it's a really nice idea, but are you sure you want to memorize all those lines? And what if they pick some really ugly Joseph?" Only my little sister, Jessica, spoke the truth, "You as Mary???? You'll never get that part!!" Larry kicked her under the table, and Mom gave her a dirty look.

They used every technique they knew to try to talk me out of it, but their reluctance only made me more determined. I had this "now or never" feeling—if I didn't make my move this year, I was in danger of spending the rest of my life hiding out with the sheep.

I have to give my family credit. Once they realized they couldn't talk me out of this, they really came through for me. Every night at the dinner table they listened to me practice. Every morning I got up early to practice, reciting my lines to Grandpa when he was shaving. After school I bugged my brother till he read Joseph's part for me. We had an agreement—he'd help out as long as I promised never to ask him when his friends were around. Even Jessica turned off her cartoons long enough to listen. By the time the audition came, everyone in my family knew those words inside-out, and upside-down, and in their sleep, even the "big speech" known as "The Magnificat".

There were three girls trying out for Mary, and I was the last to go up on the stage. Sheri Bender went first, but you could tell from the way she walked up there that she wanted no part in this. Her sister had played Mary five years before, and her parents seemed to think it would be nice if it became a family tradition. Her heart wasn't in it.

Next came Joannie Cook. Everyone was expecting her to get the part. After all, she had played the Angel Gabriel the year before, and we all knew that Gabriel was a stepping stone to the starring role of Mary. She walked on stage with confidence, shooting a knowing look to her section of the audience, a massive group of family and friends. My heart sank a little. Joannie did an okay job, however she was a lot more nervous than I thought she would be. She stumbled over a few words and left out a whole section from the big speech. Mrs. Seldon smiled when she was done and said, "That's alright,

Joannie, you've got two months to practice your speech."

Then it was my turn. I projected my voice to the back of the room, breathing from my diaphragm as the speech teacher at school had taught. My pronunciation and diction were perfect. I paused at just the right places, matching my actions to my words, and I even spoke with feeling. There was a hushed silence when I finished. Then Joannie Cook burst into tears and ran out of the room, and Mrs. Seldon congratulated me on getting the part of Mary, mother of Jesus. My family was stunned, at a loss for words. So we stopped at Ben and Jerry's on the way home to have something to do with our mouths.

We began rehearsing after Sunday School every week for the next seven weeks, and then every afternoon the week before the Christmas pageant. I grew more and more confident, and everyone agreed that this was going to be the best pageant ever.

Finally, pageant night arrived. I got to the church two hours early, because Mrs. Seldon said it would take that long to get my costume just right. I wore a pale blue cotton robe with a tie around the waist. Joleen spent a half-hour getting my headdress perfect—so that exactly one inch of my hair was visible. The make-up took even longer; the lady who drives the big pink Cadillac to church tried four different shades of blush before she thought I looked holy enough to be the mother of Our Savior. All the time they fussed over me, I stood calmly, reciting my lines over and over in my head. I must have said the "big speech" twenty times during those two hours.

When they were finally done, I had a few moments to peek through the curtain before the show began. The sanctuary was packed. I picked out my family: my mom in her brand new dress, Grandpa with his favorite bow tie, Larry in the sports coat I'd only seen him wear once before, and Jessica in her red velvet dress. The whole row was filled with family and friends who had come to see my debut: my Godmother Donna, my Aunt Kathleen and Uncle Steven and my cousins Eric and Joseph. I was about to poke my head out and wave to them, when Mrs. Seldon pulled me back. It was time to go on.

The first half of the pageant went just as we had rehearsed. The Angel Gabriel spoke to me, and I responded with the grace and faithfulness you would expect from the one who was selected to give birth to a savior. The angel whispered in Joseph's ear too, inspiring a gallant speech about how he would stand by me. The sheep were contently grazing and the multitude of angels were behaving, well, like angels. Joseph and I journeyed down the long center aisle to our hometown of Bethlehem, worrying over the lack of affordable housing, giving thanks to God for a humble stable, and then making a little blond-haired baby doll appear out of nowhere.

Then it was time for the "big speech"—the one in which I, the mother of the Prince of Peace, praised God for this beautiful child, this baby boy who never cried, and who gave nothing but joy to his blessed parents, and would save the world. As I had done so many Sunday afternoons this fall, I leaned over to the manger to pick up the baby doll, but before I could open my mouth to begin my speech, a real baby began to cry.

Along with everyone else in the room, I looked toward the sound. In the seventh pew on the right-hand side, there was a young man holding an infant, a little baby dressed in pink who couldn't have been more than two months old. I could see from the look of panic on the man's face that he had no idea what to do. He was trapped in the middle of a long pew, surrounded by large adults on each side. He couldn't get out without making a huge commotion. And he couldn't comfort his child without getting up to walk around.

His panic, I'm sure, was intensified by the collective gasp he heard from the crowd, and the disapproving stares coming at him like hundreds of little swords. Clearly he was new to our community, and he hadn't known that babies were not welcome at this pageant to commemorate the birth of the baby Jesus. He sat there frozen, while his baby screamed louder and louder.

Out of the corner of my eye, I saw Mrs. Seldon motioning to me, and suddenly I remembered the rule she had hammered into us during our months of rehearsal; if there is a distraction, ignore it and keep going. I turned away from the crying baby, focused on the silent baby doll in my arms and tried to remember my speech. It was gone. I looked at my brother, who was making funny expressions with his mouth. I finally realized he was trying to mouth the words for me, but it just looked like he was chewing too many wads of bubble gum. I looked at Mrs. Seldon; I looked at Joseph; I looked at the floor. The words were nowhere to be found. Meanwhile, the baby in the seventh pew screamed louder than ever.

I don't know how to explain what happened next. Maybe my instincts as a big sister or a babysitter kicked in. Without a word, I handed Joseph the blond baby doll, walked down the aisle to the seventh pew, squeezed my way past eight or ten knees until I got to the terrorized man with the screaming baby. I held out my hands, and without blinking an eye, the man handed his child to me. I pushed my way back through the sea of knees.

I knew exactly what this screaming baby needed—someone to walk with her and sing to her. My eyes rested, just for a moment, on that makeshift cradle sitting on the chancel surrounded by straw, and as I walked up and down the aisle, I began to sing in her ear—"Away in a manger, no crib for a bed...." By the time "the little Lord Jesus laid down his sweet head," the screaming died down to a whimper—soft enough, I guess, that it no longer drowned out my singing. When I started in on "the stars in the sky," I realized I wasn't singing alone—my Godmother Donna was singing with me, and then my aunt and uncle and cousins, and my brother and sister and grandpa. We got to the end of the carol and the baby was cooing to the music.

Before I could head back to the seventh pew, my mom started in on my favorite carol, *O Little Town of Bethlehem*. I held the baby and rocked her and sang. Joseph joined in, then Sheri Bender and Joannie Cook and the baby's greatly relieved dad. I don't know who started the next carol, or the next one, or the one after that. They just happened. By this time even the sheep were lowing. In the middle of *Silent Night*, I looked down and saw the baby was sleeping. Then I looked up and saw Mrs. Seldon looking at the baby with tears streaming down her cheeks. I couldn't be sure, but it looked like she was singing, too.

I was the one who started the last carol—"What child is this, who laid to rest, on Mary's lap is sleeping?" When we got to the chorus, I returned to that seventh pew climbed past the knees, and handed the baby to her father. Then I nodded to Joseph, and we walked down the aisle and out of the sanctuary, followed by a multitude of angels and shepherds and kings. The pageant was over; the story of the Christ child born again into the hearts of the world had been told.

The Magnificat: Luke 1:47-55
"Mary's Big Speech"

And Mary said,
'My soul magnifies the Lord,
and my spirit rejoices in God my Savior,
for He has looked with favor on the lowliness of His servant.
Surely, from now on all generations will call me blessed.
For the Mighty One has done great things for me,
and Holy is His name.
His mercy is for those who fear him
from generation to generation.
He has shown strength with his arm.
He has scattered the proud in the thoughts of their hearts.
He has brought down the powerful from their thrones,
and lifted up the lowly.
He has filled the hungry with good things,
and sent the rich away empty.
He has helped His servant Israel,
in remembrance of His mercy,
according to the promise He made to our ancestors,
to Abraham and to his descendants forever.'

BURLAP AND SATIN

by S. Lindy Purdy

I am turning the page on my calendar today. The pages went by so fast this year, and now we begin December. Funny thing about December, December gets its name from the Latin word decem (meaning ten) because it was originally the tenth month of the year in the Roman calendar. But in our Gregorian calendar, it became the twelfth month. For me, December means Christmas.

What I like most about Christmas is—the children's pageant. What I fear most about Christmas is—the children's pageant. Every year about this time, the dread of "pageant season" hits me. I can't believe it is already here, it seems like school has just started! Then, each year after it is over, I sit a while with the images of angels with crooked halos, of Magi tripping on their long robes, the proud Marys and serious Josephs, cattle and sheep lowing and waving to an appreciative section of the audience. Each year I sit in the afterglow and chuckle at the near disaster that always accompanies the yearly pageant. Like the time Mr. Adams made beautiful wooden staffs for all the shepherds, and Sam and Kyle noticed that they looked a lot like hockey sticks. You can imagine the rest!! Or the year that Mrs. Stanford brought grape drink for refreshments on the night of the performance and Joseph looked like he had a purple perma-smile.

Well, it's pageant season again. Bah, Humbug!

But, ahhh, there's a hint of snow in the air, can you feel it? Did you notice how bright the stars are against the dark winter sky? I even caught myself humming "Pah Rum Pah Pum Pum" this morning. It is "pageant season" again.

There it is. Can you see it? Over there in the corner, that dull brown heap. Someone threw a Pilgrim hat and some high black boots over it, but it is plenty visible. There it is, that scrappy pile of scratchy burlap, tossed carelessly in the corner of the costume closet. Do you see it? Burlap, whoever invented burlap must have been in a bad mood, or in a real hurry. I dread the burlap. To make it worse, right next to that drab, brown tangle of burlap, hangs the elegant satin; a long row of shiny white satin robes, neatly hung, with angel wings, and sparkly halos draped between.

And next to the angel costumes, the majestic, deep red and purple satin gowns reserved for the pageant Magi, or as Jason said last year—the wise guys. Even the furry brown cow capes have some appeal compared to the crumpled burlap.

Burlap, the costume of shepherds. Burlap, quickly sewn together into pull-over tunics that cover the jeans and sweatshirts of the pageant shepherds. Burlap, is rough and ugly—and it smells. You know that burlap smell! It makes me sneeze! But I suppose it is fitting.

At the time of Jesus, shepherding was a common career; herding sheep was an important industry. Shepherds spent all of their time taking care of their sheep, herding them from place to place to find food, even sleeping outside with their sheep at night. Sheep are not the most pleasant smelling animals to hang around with, so when shepherds came into town, they were dirty, sweaty and smelly. The tradesmen in town and at the market places were polite to them, the shopkeepers would wait on them, but everybody was glad when the shepherds returned to their flocks in the distant hills. Come to think of it, I guess scratchy, smelly burlap is the perfect fit for the shepherds.

But the angels, the pageant's angels, get to wear those shiny satin robes, with wings and sparkly halos. Satin is soft and beautiful—and clean. Angels are otherworldly, swooping and bending, even though they are often running and jumping when it comes time for the pageant. Makes me wonder though, the first words that angels say in the Bible are "Do not be afraid," or "Fear Not!" White satin swooping little girls in satin robes are hardly anything to be afraid of. Do you remember when the Angel Gabriel swoops down to Mary, the first words he says are, "Do not be afraid Mary, you have found favor with God. I bring you Good News of Great Joy!"

I guess that could be pretty scary when you think about what the good news was. Mary, she must have been just barely in her teens, and an angel appears and tells her

"The child that will be born to you will be called holy, The Son of God." That is scary news even when it is delivered by angelic, satiny cherubs. Ah, The Pageant.

I don't know how you do your pageant, but at my church there are tryouts and rehearsals for the speaking parts; Mary and Joseph and the Angel Gabriel. There is usually some subtle competition for these parts—from the parents. I get a lot of advice on who should be Mary each year, and some subtle or not so subtle pressure about who deserves the role.

I can usually sense which of the fourth and fifth grade girls is campaigning for the part of Mary by the time our All Church Picnic rolls around in September. Their moms are dropping comments, just loud enough for me to hear. "Maggie has become such a young lady, and her voice is so lovely. She would be so perfect for the part of Mary in the Christmas Pageant this year." "Sally has been taking voice lessons all summer, she is so excited to be Mary in the pageant."

It is always a difficult choice, and the not-chosen Mary's generally vie for the part of the Angel Gabriel, or Gabriella as the case may be. One year, we had three girls; all good friends vying for those parts. We ended up having angel Gabriella twins.

We also hold auditions for the parts of the Magi and the Inn Keeper. I remember the year that Joey Anderson was one of the Magi, and he looked inside his gift box at the pitiful lump of Myrrh and felt so sad for Baby Jesus and added one of his prized Matchbox cars. Only his younger brother, Jason, thought it was his matchbook car, and was not so glad to share it, even with Baby Jesus.

I guess we are fortunate. Stan Barrows always reads the part of the narrator, and he helps with the rehearsals for the speaking parts. The angels and shepherds just need to show up for the final rehearsal and stable animals just show up on the day of the pageant and put on a costume.

There are plenty of kids, mostly little girls, who come early to stake out an angel costume for the pageant. So there are always multitudes of angels, literally flurries of white satin. Sara Janecky spends a whole day bending and straightening all the halos—in hopes that the angels will appear more regal. But as soon as they are pulled on to heads, they look more like television antennas. I remember the year that Melissa Conners brought a magic wand to go with her angel costume. When the Inn Keeper announced that there was no room at the Inn, she waved that wand like crazy and shouted the words, "Abra Cadabra make a room appear." She totally scared the next words right out of the Inn Keeper, and Joseph finally said, "Hey Mary, let's just go sleep in the shed."

Shepherds are more reluctant. Shepherds take some convincing. They just don't seem to want to pull that scratchy, smelly burlap on, and tie scarves around their heads. Shepherds are usually the toughest role to cast. When you think about it, angels get satin and clouds and the Hallelujah Chorus for props. Shepherds get burlap, taped together staffs, and a stable with straw.

But isn't that the story that we celebrate? Mary and Joseph, and the baby Jesus, surrounded by satin and burlap. The most important baby in the world, born a King, a Savior, in a smelly, scratchy stable. Jesus—waited for, longed for, predicted by prophets, and proclaimed by angels, "Unto you a child is born, unto you a son is given; and the government shall be upon his shoulders, and his name shall be Wonderful Counselor, Mighty God, Everlasting Father, Prince of Peace." A humble birth, but with a multitude of heavenly angels singing "Glory to God in the highest, Emmanuel, God with us."

And it came to pass that there was no room at the Inn. Jesus was placed in an animal-feeding trough, in a stable, because there was no room at the inn. Why would the beloved Son of God enter life in this lowly place, at the margin of human existence, at the edge of society, in obscurity? No grand chariot brandishing swords and shields, no mighty winds, no trumpets blaring, no majestic words from on high, no grand palace, or parades, or parties.

None of that, just a smelly, scratchy stable. The angel multitudes did not even attend Jesus' birth; their heavenly proclamation came in the fields, to the sweaty shepherds.

Burlap and Satin

"Fear not: for, behold, I bring you good tidings of great joy, which shall be to all people. For unto you is born this day in the city of David a Savior, which is Christ the Lord." And the shepherds said to one another, "Let us go now to Bethlehem and see this thing that has taken place, which the Lord has made known to us." This may seem incredible, but there it is. It is ironic that shepherds were the first to seek out the baby Jesus, and then later in life, Jesus would call himself a shepherd, the Good Shepherd.

It makes me wonder. I think God wanted to be perfectly clear. God came for e-v-e-r-y-o-n-e. God's good news of great joy is for all people. God comes into the scratchy, dark corners of our lives, not just the clean and shiny places. God knows about desperateness and loneliness and rejection. God knows that we may want satin, but often we must wear burlap. We long for the life that the angels proclaim; to be loved by God, actually loved by God, in spite of ourselves. And we discover that God reaches out to us in all times, in all places, whether we are clothed in silky satin or scratchy burlap. God sees us at our worst, and offers us the best.

We love satin, but we need burlap, or we might just miss the true lesson of Christmas. As the angels said to the shepherds, "Glory to God in the highest and on earth peace, goodwill toward all people."

Luke 2:8-20

In that region there were shepherds living in the fields, keeping watch over their flock by night. Then an angel of the Lord stood before them, and the glory of the Lord shone around them, and they were terrified. But the angel said to them, 'Do not be afraid; for see—I am bringing you good news of great joy for all the people: to you is born this day in the city of David a Saviour, who is the Messiah, the Lord. This will be a sign for you: you will find a child wrapped in bands of cloth and lying in a manger.' And suddenly there was with the angel a multitude of the heavenly host, praising God and saying, 'Glory to God in the highest heaven, and on earth peace among those whom he favors!'

When the angels had left them and gone into heaven, the shepherds said to one another, 'Let us go now to Bethlehem and see this thing that has taken place, which the Lord has made known to us.' So they went with haste and found Mary and Joseph, and the child lying in the manger. When they saw this, they made known what had been told them about this child; and all who heard it were amazed at what the shepherds told them. But Mary treasured all these words and pondered them in her heart. The shepherds returned, glorifying and praising God for all they had heard and seen, as it had been told them.

LIGHT UP THE WORLD

by S. Lindy Purdy

Have you ever heard of "magic candles?" I think you might want to hear this story. My name is Fran Wick and my husband Stan and I are the proprietors of The Waxford Wick Company in Waxford, Minnesota, "Home of The Magic Candle." Have you been to Waxford? It's west of Hackensack on County Road 42, just past Rudy's Bait and Bakery and the Pack-A-Snack. I must admit it is a small, small town. Population thirty seven, expectantly waiting to be thirty eight.

I am excited to tell you about our candles. They are not just any kind of candles; they are magic candles. No, they aren't those crazy candles that you cannot blow out. They don't melt down and reveal some secret message. But they are magic indeed.

The story of the magic candles begins back about 10 years ago. Stan was a mail carrier in Hubbard County and I worked for the Department of Natural Resources, testing the water quality of lakes and streams in Western Minnesota.

Stan delivered mail to the rural routes west of Park Rapids, where our town of Waxford is located. Every morning he drove to the city of Park Rapids at about 3:00 a.m. to pick up the mail sacks and then head out to the country. He delivered to Snellman and Wolf Lake and Ponsford and Osage, but he also delivered to resorts, convenience stores, homes and even churches along the way. I often went with him, to take water samples.

On one of those trips, I saw one of the most amusing things. On West Lake Road, just outside of Pennington, Mr. George Brown had two mailboxes. One was at the regular height and the other was 20 feet up in the air with a big sign hanging on it saying, "Air Mail." There was not even a landing strip for the airplanes. What a joke!

Well, I was with Stan on his route when the idea of candle-making was first ignited. It had been a long day. It was just a few days before Christmas, which always required extra deliveries with more mail and packages than usual. We had been out to the far western edge of the route and were headed back to Waxford. Our last delivery was to Howard's Hardware Haven, and we had several packages on board. When we finally arrived, there was Reverend Burnet. He was waiting for an important package and we were at least two hours later than usual.

We unloaded the van. There was a box with 3M gadgets, a shipment of snow scrapers, some sundry nuts and bolts, but no shipment from the Charleston Candle Company. There was only a postcard that Reverend Burnet read out loud with great disappointment: "#33408, 6" taper—Out of Stock." Out of stock. No explanation. It turned out that Reverend Burnet was planning some fancy Christmas Eve service at his church, the Osage Community Church, and it was only two days away.

It was Wednesday, and he was so hoping to have the candles that day so he could have the Busy Hands Women's Guild get them ready for Friday's service. He looked so crestfallen, so defeated. Stan and I were not churchgoing people—we never really thought we were missing anything. But when we saw the look of disappointment on Reverend Burnet's face, we were moved.

The word "candle" instantly triggered a thought. My sister Nan and I had made candles when we were in high school to give to our family and friends for Christmas. It was kind of fun. So, I casually asked Reverend Burnet just how many candles he would need. I stepped back a bit when he replied, "I ordered twelve dozen." I quickly calculated 144 candles—that was a lot more candles than Nan and I had ever made those many years ago.

I don't know what got into me, and Stan was stunned when he heard, "Reverend Burnet, we can get you those candles by Friday morning" come out of my mouth.

I could see the look of relief spread across Reverend Burnet's face, and the look of panic break out on Stan's. "Can you describe the candles that you need?" I asked. Well, that was the birth of the Waxford Wick "magic candles."

What was I thinking? That first order, or gesture of goodwill, was nearly a disaster. On the way home, Stan and I stopped at almost every town within driving distance to scrounge up the supplies we needed. I hadn't thought about the fact that it was three days before Christmas and the stores would be busy and the shelves nearly bare.

We got much of what we needed in Park Rapids, but even after all our stops, we were still short of wicks, (not including us Wicks), and we couldn't find any wax hardener. It felt like we were defeated before we had even begun. But we were determined not to let Reverend Burnet down. We would have to improvise.

We finally arrived back home at 10:30 that evening, exhausted but determined. I climbed up into the storage area over our garage, trying to locate those candle-making supplies from years ago. I never throw stuff like that away. I found a treasure trove of projects left from our early years of marriage. We had no money, so we gave "home-made" gifts for Christmas. I sure loved those days. I kept every hand-crocheted trivet, years of plaster of paris handprints, the macaroni-decorated picture frames, and a macramé plant hanger.

I finally found the box labeled "Candle-making," behind the decoupage supplies, and dragged it out with the macramé twine, which I sure hoped would work for the candle wicks. When I got the box down to the kitchen, I realized that there was not one thing in that box that would help us with this new project. The wax had melted into a mass that was hard as a rock and yellowed with age, there was only a few feet of wick left, and the stuff we used for hardener had turned to a gummy mess and was not very appealing. I took a whiff—it smelled just like the soybean oil that is in abundant supply at the Grain and Green Co-op. Soybeans are a major crop around here. You can buy a gallon of the stuff for almost nothing. I began to wonder if that would work for our candles.

The bright spot was that we uncovered the old coat hanger drying racks that we had assembled many years ago. Well, it was a start. We had to try it. We got out my spaghetti pot and melted and mixed up the wax (and our secret ingredient), and then we began dipping. We decided our first experimental batch should be small, ten candles.

Have you ever dipped candles? First, you cut the wick twice as long as the candles plus two inches, then you fold the wick in half, and dangle both ends into the hot wax mixture to the desired candle length.

I remembered that we counted to ten, then ever-so-slowly lifted the double candle up out of the wax, and carefully hung it over the drying racks. We mixed in some of the macramé twine with that first batch to see if it would work. It generally takes half an hour to cure after a dip, so we set the timer to thirty minutes and waited. Then the second dip, count to ten, slowly lift, hang to dry, wait thirty minutes to set. Since each candle requires ten dips, Stan and I started calculating how long this would take—approximately six hours. By the third dip, we had made some production improvements. The ten count became five, the thirty minutes more like fifteen. Stan decided to move the drying racks to the porch for faster cooling, and that seemed to be a strategic key to our success. In three hours and twenty minutes batch number one was completed and tested. We crossed our fingers and lit a test candle. The true candle wick worked fine, better than fine, it was incredible. But the macramé wick was not so great.

Stan suggested that we pre-dip the wick in the wax, and after that refinement, we were in production. We found some old metal hangers and doubled the drying racks. Needless to say, we had no idea what we were getting ourselves into.

With only a few hours of sleep, we finished at eleven p.m. on Thursday. The next day would be Christmas Eve; the day the candles needed to be in place at Osage Community Church. We did it, the candles were ready for the big service.

Now, don't you think that those candles were magic? But the real magic came later. We delivered the candles Friday morning and found a worried and frazzled Reverend Burnet in his office. He was so relieved to see us carrying a box of candles. He had three of the church ladies sitting in waiting—well, they were pacing really. We knew them, of course, and knew that they were the kind of people that would stuff mailings, count money, bake cookies, and arrange flowers. You know the kind. I suppose every church needs them. Well they were ready to pounce on that box and get them secured into the cup holders, and ready for the service. Reverend Burnet thanked us profusely and we took off.

All afternoon we thought about those candles and wondered how Reverend Burnet planned to use them. We couldn't get them out of our minds. After supper, Stan said he was having trouble sitting still; maybe he would take a walk. I was pretty restless too. We were both feeling a little nervousness about the debut of our first endeavor into candle-making.

I looked at the clock, it was 6:40 p.m. The sign in front to the Osage Community Church said "7:00 p.m. Candlelight Service." I looked at Stan as he was putting on his coat and said, "Should we go check on our candles?" He must have been thinking the same thing, and we quickly got ready and were out the door.

Neither of us said anything on the way to the Osage Church. There was a stillness that was filled with eager anticipation. When we got to the church, we realized that we were not the only ones with a desire to see our candles in action. We found a seat on the far side, near the back, and crowded into a pew. The sun had set over an hour ago, and as the music started, the gathered crowd began to sing and move together. It was hard not to get drawn into the spirit of the evening. Reverend Burnet read from the Bible a story about kings and stars and a baby. And right at the end he said, "It was a bright light that led the wise men to Jesus, and it is Jesus who is the bright light for each of us to follow."

Then he read again from the Bible, words that Jesus himself had said. "You are the light of the world." Did you hear that? Jesus said, "You are the light of the world." You and me, we are the light of the world. Then the lights were dimmed until all we could see was the light over the cross and the two candles that were on the altar.

Reverend Burnet lit his candle, our Waxford Wick candle, from the Christ candle on the altar and started down the center aisle. As the choir started singing slowly and softly, "Silent night, holy night," Reverend Burnet lit the candle of each person on the aisle.

"All is calm, all is bright." The light started in the center, and person to person, it began to move down the rows. "Round yon virgin, mother and child." The darkened room started to glow with the soft light of candles. "Holy infant, so tender and mild."

By this time the whole congregation was singing, so softly and so tenderly, almost a whisper. "Sleep in heavenly peace." Tears had formed in my eyes. The welled-up tears made the room look a little blurry, and all the beautiful colors of the flowers and the greens, of the people with their festive attire, made it look like a kaleidoscope. "Sleep in heavenly peace." By this time the tears were falling freely—I looked around and everyone seemed to be experiencing this moment with the same deep emotion. Even Stan was standing there trying to hold back the tears. It was silent for a moment. Just the people standing, the tears flowing, the candles lighting up the darkness. All because a little baby, born a long time ago, brought light and love into the darkness of the world, and brought a smallish group of us together to experience it all over again on this cold dark night in Osage, Minnesota. Love made visible in candlelight.

I told you these candles were magic. Well, really all candles are magic. Whenever you see a candle, whenever you light a candle, remember the magic. Remember that Christ shines His Holy light into our darkness, then commands us to let our light shine so others can see again and again the magic of love. Whenever you offer a kind word, a helping hand, a gentle touch, a random smile, you bring Christ's light to the world. And the world changes for the good.

LET YOUR LIGHT SHINE
GO LIGHT UP YOUR WORLD.

MERRY CHRISTMAS

This story brought to you through
the Gospels of Matthew and Luke and from
the Waxford Wick Magic Candle Company.

Matthew 5:14-16

Jesus said, "You are the light of the world. A city built on a hill cannot be hidden. No one after lighting a lamp puts it under the bushel basket, but on the lamp stand, and it gives light to all in the house. In the same way, let your light shine before others, so that they may see your good works and give glory to your Father in heaven."

26

THE ANGEL HAROLD

by S. Lindy Purdy

Hark the Herald Angels Sing.
Glory to the Newborn King.
Peace on Earth and Mercy Mild,
God and Sinners Reconciled.

I just love that song. I know the words by heart, and just hearing the introduction gives me the shivers. What I especially love is the word, "Hark!" We don't use the word "hark" in our daily vocabulary, but I think it might be a good word for many occasions.

"Hark, dinner is ready."
"Hark, it is time for an oil change in the Toyota."
"Hark, I hear footsteps in the hall."

It makes you kind of wonder what a herald angel is. I am not sure what a herald angel is, but I want to tell you a story about Harold, the angel.

I first heard about the angel Harold from my son, Ben, when he was a pre-schooler at our church. I remember Ben coming home with wild stories about this white-haired angel that had gotten him out of one jam or another. This "angel" made his way into many of our after-school conversations.

"How was your day, Ben?"
"It was OK, the angel helped me find my jacket."
"What angel?"
"Harold."

Or

>"How was your class today, Ben?"
>"I don't know."
>"Ben, you are the only one who knows."
>"Well, when Tommy lost his football, I told him that the angel would get it back, but he didn't believe me."
>"Ben, not everyone can see angels."

Lots of kids have imaginary friends, right?—I was trying to be a good mom, so I just took this stage in stride. I didn't encourage the idea of angels, and when Ben's angel came up in conversation I went along with it. I figured that this imaginary "angel" would go the way of Ben's abandoned sippy cup. On the other hand, his well worn blankie still accompanied him to bed every night. At least angels were a healthy kind of pretend companion.

Then one day—

>"Did you have a good day at school today, Ben?"
>"Oh, it was great, the angel put up the Christmas tree."
>"The angel?"
>"Yeah, the one I've been telling you about, Mom. The angel—Harold."
>"Oh."

Just the mention of the "tree" going into place—sent me into high gear. You see, at the Pre-school Board planning meeting in August, I opened up my big mouth and said something about loving Christmas and remembering the great "pageants" we had when I was a kid. The next thing you know, I was appointed the chairperson of this year's "Tree House Room Christmas Pageant" for the nursery school.

How hard could it be, I thought. What I didn't know then, was that it was a "tradition" for the kids in the Tree House Room—the 4 and 5 year-olds, to put on the pageant for all the kids, their parents and any other member of the church community who loved watching little ones dressed up. Who wouldn't love that? So, over the years, this pageant had become a tradition that was enjoyed by the whole community. Four years earlier, the chairperson had to move the performance to Saturday to meet the growing demand.

HARK! There will be a Christmas pageant again this year.

It came to pass, that this popular event tickled the fancy of the Women's Ministry Board, so they agreed to serve cookies and milk (and coffee, of course) after the pageant. And BEHOLD (another great underused word), the church council gave a one-time grant, for some new costumes, and the Thimblebees agreed to make them! So, there I was, only three-and-a-half weeks until the big day.

Things went surprisingly well. Emmy's mom volunteered to get all the old costumes out of storage and into shape—you should have seen those burly, burlap shepherds' cloaks. They needed a good airing out and—whew! I didn't think the perma-wrinkles would ever go away. Oh well, shepherds were never known for their natty attire. There were halos to straighten, crooks to repair, and the cotton batting on the sheep costumes needed fluffing. Brady's dad agreed to get the stable out of storage and put a few extra nails in to hold it up. He even made a new manger and lined it with straw.

I dug out the folder from the year before, only to discover that the script was penciled over with corrections and changes, and pages two and three were missing. Well, how hard could it be to re-write—I knew where the story came from—but where was my Bible? Well, if I couldn't find mine, I knew who had one. Pastor John—he probably had Bibles to spare.

Within a week, everyone was busy and things were on track. Mrs. Rogers, the Tree House teacher, was in charge of casting. Every one of her students would have a part. She selected Taylor's dad to be the narrator, because he was a weather man in real life and he had a great deep voice. He would be the voice, and by design the only voice of the pageant. MacKenzie's mom agreed to play the piano and Lauren, a high school student, volunteered to do the sound effects—you know the clomping of the donkey feet, the stable door opening, the swoosh of angel wings, whatever. She did it the year before and frankly, I think she invented that part for herself after attending a performance of The Prairie Home Companion.

My job was Director, which basically meant getting everyone on stage at the right time. I was just glad that I didn't have to dole out the parts—there would be a lot of disappointed Mary-wanna-bes, I knew that. The roles were assigned a week before the performance, and Ben would be one of the three wisemen. He was not too crazy about the tall, tippy hat that went with his costume, but he was excited to have a gift to give to baby Jesus.

In retrospect, two casting mistakes were made; giving Colin, the aspiring golfer, a shepherd's staff, and assigning Andrew the part of Joseph. Andrew was in his girls-have-germs stage, and he refused to take Mary's hand or even stand near her. But all in all, as the day came for the pageant, there were smiling angels and contented but busy sheep. Celia was selected to be Mary, and her family, all 27 of them, came an hour early to secure the first three rows.

The younger kids in the pre-school started the program singing "Away in a Manger" and "Jingle Bells." Mrs. Rogers welcomed the audience and thanked all the volunteers and the pageant was underway.

The stage was set, Mary and Joseph standing in their places. Stage left, the angel was ready to swoop in, Lauren was ready with the sound effects, and the narrator began:

"The Birth of Jesus."

"Now the birth of Jesus the Messiah took place in this way. An angel, sent by God, came to a young girl named Mary." [SWOOP, Lauren was ready with the sound effects] "The heralding angel proclaimed, 'Greetings, favored one. Do not be afraid Mary, for you have found favor with God. You will give birth to a son, and you will name him Jesus. He will be great, and will be called the Son of the Most High.'"

"Now, Mary was already engaged to Joseph, and the wedding would be soon. What an amazing and impossible message the angel brought to this young girl. But even more amazing and impossible was that Mary looked at the angel and said, 'Be it unto me according to your word.' Joseph loved Mary very much, but when he heard about the baby, he was confused."

[SWOOP] "The angel of the Lord appeared also to Joseph saying, 'Joseph, son of David, do not be afraid to take Mary as your wife, for she shall give birth to a son, and you are to name him Jesus, for he will save his people.'" It makes you wonder about angels when the first words they say are "Do not be afraid!"

The narrator continued, "In those days a decree went out from Emperor Augustus that all the world should be registered, each in his own town. Joseph also went from the town of Nazareth in Galilee to Judea, to the city of David called Bethlehem, because he was descended from the house and family of David. He went to be registered with Mary."

Mary and Joseph began to walk slowly toward the stable scene, guided and pushed a little by a dad in donkey garb—[CLIP, CLOP, CLIP, CLOP].

"The little town of Bethlehem was crowded, overcrowded with people coming to be registered for the first census when Quirinius was governor of Syria. There was no room in the inn, no place to take Mary, and the time came for her to deliver her child. Finally, they were guided to a stable." [CREAK—DOOR OPENING] "It was there in that stable that Mary gave birth to her firstborn son and wrapped him in swaddling clothes and laid him in the manger."

At that moment, Celia/"Mary" took one look into the manger and exclaimed, "Somebody stole the baby Jesus!" And sure enough, Megan's baby doll, who was playing the part of Jesus, was not in the manger. Hearing those words, Megan, in her angel robe with wings askew and halo perched on the top of her head, came running out of the multitude, right up to the manger with tears streaming down her face. The flock of lambs who had been patiently waiting in their fields (stage right) stood to see what was happening and edged closer to the action. The shepherds couldn't keep watch over their flocks any longer, and Robbie, the tallest shepherd, saw his mom in the third row and went running. By this time, the host of heavenly angels were swarming the manger and Julia was comforting Megan, promising to share her own doll.

The narrator was looking pleadingly at me, for what to do next. I tried to motion for him to just keep reading, but with my hand signal, the three Kings assumed that it was time to make their way to Bethlehem. They arrived before the star, and leave it to Ben to notice. "Hey, where is the star?" Quickly Brad, the star-raiser, shot the star up with its long pole and it swung back and forth over the empty manger. A few parents gasped, most were on their feet by now. The middle king tripped over Colin's staff, which he was using as a three wood, and his chest of frankincense, filled with Cheerios, spilled out all over Mary and Joseph.

By this time, the stage was in chaos. I had managed to get all the kids on stage, some even got speaking parts that were not scripted, and I had a speechless narrator who would probably find reporting on a hurricane tame after this assignment.

Mrs. Rogers and I rushed onto the scene just trying to calm the Christmas chaos, when out from behind the set came a tall slender man with snow white hair, carrying a beautiful baby doll wrapped in bands of cloth. The light reflected from his shining white hair and the white cloths around the baby caught a shaft of light from the overhead windows—it was an eerie sight. The words "Do not be afraid" came to mind. I recognized the man. Mr. Crandall was one of the buildings and grounds crew at the church, but he seemed transformed somehow.

The kids began to settle, and all eyes were on this gentle man, moving slowly toward the center of the stage. With each step he took, the crowd grew quieter and quieter. All eyes were fixed on him, especially Megan's, as this giant slowly lowered baby Jesus into the waiting manger.

As he stood up again, he spoke these words, "But the angel said to them, 'Do not be afraid: for see, I am bringing you good news of great joy for all the people; to you is born this day a Savior, who is the Messiah, the Lord.' "

And suddenly, there was with the angel a multitude of the heavenly hosts, little girls in white smocks giggling and googling over the miraculous baby Jesus, angel wings fluttering; proud Mary and shy Joseph beaming, lambs cooing, shepherds and wisemen cheering. When from the background the music started, Mrs. Rogers stepped forward inviting everyone to stand and sing—"Silent Night, Holy Night, All is calm, All is bright."

What a holy and sacred chaos! What a message of good news and great joy. That is how I will remember the glorious and impossible message of God's incarnation, through the joy and wonder on the faces of the children when Jesus came. Glory to God in the highest, and on earth peace and goodwill toward all people.

To this day, I do not know how baby Jesus disappeared, I suspect it was the swooping angel who couldn't resist the temptation of hugging that special baby. Oh, and by the way, Ben had the last word that day. It was in the car on the way home after the smiles and hugs, the high-fives and three helpings of cookies and milk, that he said to me, "See mom, the angel Harold found baby Jesus. I knew he would."

May the magic and wonder of this season transform you from within, as you experience again Emmanuel, "God with us."

Luke 2:10-12
But the angel said to them, "Do not be afraid: for see—I am bringing you good news of great joy for all the people: to you is born this day in the city of David a Savior, who is the Messiah, the Lord. This will be a sign for you: you will find a child wrapped in bands of cloth and lying in a manger."

CHRISTMAS CAROL

by S. Lindy Purdy

I have a friend, Carol. I have known Carol all of my life, and almost all of hers. You see our moms were best friends in high school. Carol is 5 months, 3 days older than I am, and the stories of our antics as kids are etched into my childhood memories. Maybe the first thing you need to know about Carol is that she was very organized, and maybe a little bossy. She was always the one with the plan, and the rest of us followed.

On the other hand, I have always loved the thrill of the moment. I love to run ahead, to think on my feet, to go with the flow. Sometimes these traits get me into hot water, but that's a story for another day. I want to tell you about Carol. No, I need to tell you about Carol, because this year I finally understand.

Carol was born on December 25, on her grandmother Joy's birthday. Now some people would lament that date, sharing your birthday with the world, combined birthday and Christmas gifts, etc. But Carol loved it. In fact, she just plain loved Christmas and everything about it. Carol claimed that she was named especially for Christmas, that she was an original "Christmas Carol." She knew all the favorite Christmas carols by heart. She especially loved Silent Night, which she sang year round. Carol collected all the catalogs that came in the fall mail, and she began preparing her list for Santa right around Halloween. Long before December, she decorated everything in sight with red and green and lights and holly. Some of those decorations stayed up all year long.

But there was one Christmas, many years ago, with the most incredible Christmas pageant that I want to tell you about. Carol and I were in second grade and the second grade Sunday School class was always assigned to the role of the shepherds for the annual pageant.

Mrs. Hallberg was our teacher that year, and how fortunate we were! Mrs. Hallberg was the director of the high school drama club, and she wanted our performance to be the best of all the grades. The shepherds would shine, Mrs. Hallberg promised. We had one speaking line and three acting moments in the annual Christmas pageant.

We started working on our parts during the second week in November, five weeks before the performance. First, Mrs. Hallberg worked with our class on the actions; the facial expressions and gestures needed by the members of the shepherd cast. You remember the story, "In that region there were shepherds living in the fields, keeping watch over their flock by night. Then the angel of the Lord stood before them, and the glory of the Lord shone around them, and they were terrified." So the class practiced that look of being terrified—terrified by a sixth grade angel. Joey was particularly good at this, because he had twin sisters in the sixth grade, and he was terrified that they would get the part of the twin angels.

So we practiced terrified. Have you noticed that in the Bible, the appearance of angels is often terrifying? People needed to be soothed and reassured when an angel appeared on the scene. Well, I guess it would be terrifying if an extra-terrestrial appeared out of nowhere, in a flash of light, right before my eyes, "Lindy, I am the angel of the Lord!" Ahh! Terrified! Try it. Hunker down your shoulder, furl your eye-brows, grit your teeth, lean back and look terrified. Well, we practiced that look as a class until we had it down pat.

As the shepherd's part of the story continues, the angel reassures the shepherds, "Do not be afraid; for see—I am bringing you good news of great joy for all people; to you is born this day in the city of David a savior, who is the Messiah, the Lord." Born this day, a baby, a brand new, wiggling, smiling, cooing baby, wrapped all up in swaddling cloths. Can you imagine—no zippers, or snaps, or Velcro, just a soft, cuddly wrap. Mrs. Hallberg demonstrated this design using a long strip of soft polar fleece and Jenny's baby doll. Of course we all wanted to try this out—at least the girls did.

The angel's message about a baby was our cue as the second grade shepherds to change our terrified expression to one of amazement. That meant raising our eyebrow slightly and leaving our mouths slightly ajar with eyes wide. Back then I had to practice that look of amazement, which sometimes made me look like I was being tortured, but these days, it comes naturally. I am frequently amazed by what God is doing, especially when a baby is involved.

So we mastered "terrified", then "amazed". Later in that scene, you know the one that Luke writes about, the shepherds finally see some action. They gather together and say to one another, "Let us go now to Bethlehem and see this thing that has taken place, which the Lord has made known to us."

It was George's idea to gather together and make a huddle. After all, he was the one who loved football so much that he wore his Minnesota Vikings jersey almost every day. Well, it seemed like a good idea, and Mrs. Hallberg agreed, so we gathered around, hands encircling our huddled group, to recite our one line. Mrs. Hallberg edited the line slightly so we could actually learn it and almost say it together, "Let's go to Bethlehem to see the baby Jesus." All together now, "Let's go to Bethlehem to see the baby Jesus." It was almost like we were the shepherd troop.

Then Luke's story actually says, "So they went with haste." So our next move was to quickly move from the fields at stage left, across the chancel to stage right where Mary and Joseph were sitting "amazed," next to the babe lying in the manger.

Again we used our practiced expressions of amazement as we circled the holy family, silently mouthing words that signified the shepherds sharing the good news about this miraculous event. Do you remember? This is the part where Luke tells us that "Mary treasured all these words and pondered them in her heart." I love that part.

We circled the manger scene twice and headed back to where we came from. Our third moment of expression—moved to glorifying and praising God for all that had happened. Arms up and down with hands in praying position. When you think of it, the shepherds really are the stars of the story. At least second to Mary and Joseph and Jesus. After all, when Jesus grew up, he called himself the Good Shepherd. And we found out that it takes a lot of acting and expression to be a shepherd.

Well, no one took it more seriously than Carol. She set up some practice sessions of her own and asked my mom to help in between our Sunday rehearsals. By the time of the performance, we had it down pat—terrified, amazed, praising and glorifying.

It came to the afternoon of the actual pageant, and the shepherds were ready, we were psyched! We had the coolest smocks and sashes and head scarves that were made new that year by the Women's Guild, and Kevin's dad made staffs for each of us out of willow branches. The rest of the cast was ready too it seemed, but we were really prepared. We were bound to captivate the appreciative audience. Kate and Ellie even came up with a cheer that we would do in our classroom/dressing room before assembling with the rest of the kids in the pageant:

> *Shepherds Rock, Shepherds Rock Yea, Ra Ra, Shepherds!*
> (as we lifted our crooks high with anticipation)

This was our big day, the stars of the Christmas pageant were ready to go. What could go wrong? We had thought it out. We had practiced it thoroughly. We knew our cues. We had Mrs. Hallberg—and we had Christmas Carol.

That surely was a Christmas pageant to remember. Twenty-two years ago. After that, Carol's family moved away. Our moms remained friends and they saw each other on occasion, but I lost track of Carol. Each year, the Christmas pageant reminded me of Carol. Over the years, I worked my way up from shepherd to shining star, to wise man and finally, before I left Christmas pageants to the little kids, to the scary angel.

This year it is me teaching second grade Sunday School and my own daughter will be one of the shepherds in this year's Christmas pageant.

The memories have been flooding back. The pageant of so many years ago. That day that made such an impression on me. Mrs. Hallberg our teacher, so earnest in her efforts to make us the best shepherds ever, our snappy little shepherds cheer, our shepherd huddle, George in his Vikings jersey; but especially our Christmas Carol. I wondered most about Carol. You see, the pageant went on that day, but not quite as planned and rehearsed and practiced—for Carol was missing! We waited as long as we could to do our shepherds cheer, we had her shepherd duds ready for a last minute entrance, but finally we had to go to the fields without her.

We were terrified right on cue, then amazed, we "made haste" to Bethlehem and circled the Christ Child, and we were getting ready to glorify and praise . . . when Carol came bursting into the sanctuary, tears streaming down her face as she ran up to join us. Lauren gave her a shepherd's scarf and a spontaneous huddle happened right there in the middle of the journey back to the flock.

The wisemen were thrown off a little on their entrance, but they made their way to the holy family—and alongside them was one teary shepherd. As they lay their gifts of Gold and Frankincense and Myrrh at the side of the manger, the shepherd leaned down and kissed the Christ Child's cheek, and whispered something in his ear. The angel hovering near just barely heard her say, "Jesus, I know you will love having a grandma, and my grandma Joy is the best grandma in the whole world."

I'm not sure I understood way back then, and I surely did not know how important that pageant was. But, I still remember the shepherd's response to God's breaking into the world in the form of a little baby. They were terrified, they were amazed, they responded with adoration and praise.

Christmas Carol understood that back in second grade, and maybe I do now. Christmas is about the eternal joy of a special birth, a message from God, delivered in person. Nothing can separate us from God's love. Not angels or rulers or things present or things to come, or anything else can keep God's love away from us.

This Christmas season, may we be a little terrified, or at least startled when we hear the story of God breaking into the world and into our lives. Let us be amazed by a God who seeks to be "God with us"—Emmanuel, and let us return to our own lives with adoration and praise for the One who loves us more than we can ever imagine.

Luke 2:8-9
In that region there were shepherds living in the fields, keeping watch over their flock by night. Then an angel of the Lord stood before them and the glory of the Lord shone around them and they were terrified.

HOLLY AND IVY

by S. Lindy Purdy

It is hard to believe that it's time again to think about Christmas! The dishes from Thanksgiving dinner are still warm from the dishwasher—but I feel I must tell you my life-changing story.

By the way, my name is Holly, and right now, I am snowed under—under a blanket of snow that is. One thing is obvious, it's beginning to look a lot like Christmas. I guess that's why I feel compelled to tell you this Christmas story. I already told you that my name is Holly, but in order for this story to make sense, you need to know that I have a twin sister named Ivy. Holly and Ivy, Holly and Ivy Mistletoe. And that's not all, my sister and I were born on Christmas day. The headlines of the local paper read "Joy to the World, Mr. and Mrs. Mistletoe deliver Holly and Ivy on Christmas Day." I know it is hard to believe. But just imagine the ribbing I have been taking all these years—Holly Ann Mistletoe.

You may have guessed what my mom's favorite holiday is. Mom loves Christmas. My mom loves Christmas a lot—she is the prepare-months-in-advance, decorate-every-room-of-the-house, buy-and-wrap-Christmas-gifts-before-Thanksgiving kind of Christmas lover. Half of our basement is filled with boxes of Christmas stuff stored away from January to November. (Can you identify with that?) But even amidst all the decorations and preparations, every year mom tells Ivy and me that we were her best Christmas gifts ever. Isn't that sweet? Christmas is a big deal around our house—for everyone but me, Holly Mistletoe. Until a few years ago, that is.

I told you that Ivy and I are twins, but we are far from identical. If you look at our baby picture, there I am all scowly and squinty, red-in-the-face and screaming, and Ivy is wide-eyed with her mouth gaping open, a look of utter surprise and delight. In that picture, the only thing about us that is identical is the matching red bows glued on Ivy's nearly bald head and my matted black mop.

We were quite a pair from the very start—an unmatched pair of Christmas babies. If Ivy was content to lie and watch the sparkling lights on the Christmas tree, I was hollering because that huge tree scared me. I loved to sleep with the warm sun shining on my face, and Ivy slept peacefully under the starlight. I am not quite sure when our mom and dad slept. Ivy loved to eat applesauce and oatmeal, and I apparently used it as a facial mask. I could not choke it down—I still can't. We were unique individuals from the very start. It seemed that anything to do with Christmas brought out the best in Ivy, but ended in disaster for me.

For example, the year we were one year old, our family was selected to be the Holy family for the church Christmas pageant. But what to do with twin Jesuses? I don't remember this first-hand, but this story is told every year as pageant time rolls around and it goes something like this.

We started the costume fitting process on the Friday after Thanksgiving. Mrs. Needle-nose from our church circle was the costume director and she met with us that afternoon. She was not too happy about making two sets of swaddling clothes, so it was decided that Ivy and I would share the baby Jesus duties. I would be Jesus for the 9:00 a.m. pageant, and Ivy would get all wrapped up for the 11:00 o'clock show. It would have worked out just fine, but by the time I was done with the costume, it was a wad of raveling cotton—and it did not smell too fresh either. But thankfully, Ivy was just as happy rolled up in some Bounty paper towels, and she slept through the whole thing.

Mrs. Jolliwell was assigned to watch the off-duty baby while the others were "on stage," and shortly after that pageant season, she resigned from the Board of Christian Education.

Christmas is a long season at the Mistletoe house. It starts right after summer vacation. The Mistletoe family starts ramping up for Christmas even before the retailers get their displays and commercials going. One year when my mom was in charge of making all the angel costumes for the Christmas pageant, Ivy and I had to wear angel costumes for Halloween. Boy, was that embarrassing. Ivy loved it. By the end of the night, my halo had been transformed into a Jedi lightsaber, the netting skirt was an exotic space helmet and the angel wings were wrapped under my arms and across my chest, transformed into a laser-deflecting shield. I was a Jedi warrior, a Jedi warrior princess, walking alongside a dignified angel, with a perfectly straight halo. Guess who got the most treats?

We were a Christmas-driven family. We signified Christmas. We lived for Christmas. We were the Merry Mistletoe Family. As kids, we were reminded throughout the year that Santa was comin' to town, and he was making his list. In July, if I was caught pushing someone into the swimming pool, I would hear "Holly, remember, Santa's going to 'find out who's naughty and who's nice.'" Or when eating dinner at my cousins, "you better watch out, you better not cry, you better not pout, I'm telling you why." No problem for Ivy—she was always good. I often wondered how old Santa could keep track of all those kids. Especially, Laurie Louise, yes Laurie Louise and not one syllable less. Her naughty list must have been a full time job for Santa and his spies.

I mostly tried to make sure that when I did something nice, everyone noticed, because I was sure then that Santa would know—my best chance to have more in the "nice" column than the "naughty" one. "Santa's List" was the ultimate tool for behavior control at our house.

When I got to be old enough, I figured out that "Santa" started stashing away his "good list" goodies months before Christmas. I discovered a cabinet in the basement storage room that mysteriously began to fill up right after summer vacation ended. I didn't tell Ivy till we were in 9th grade. It was fun to keep a secret from her. Once my gift list was complete and stowed in the closet, it freed me from the tyranny of "Santa's List." I figured Santa had made his tally on me for that year and I had scraped by on the positive side of the ledger. I was not a big fan of "Christmas" with all it's hoopla, but I sure liked unwrapping presents on Christmas Eve.

It was in my senior year of high school that everything changed for me. I guess that's why I need to tell you this story. You all know the story of Jesus and the way he had to curl up on a bale of straw with the animals and the angels. I have always found that to be odd. If there were so many angels, multitudes in fact, why was Jesus born in an animal-infested stable? If this Jesus came to tell us about God's love, why did he come as a speechless baby, and why in a little town like Bethlehem? Why such an ordinary, out-of-the-way beginning? This story is pretty unusual, it does make you wonder.

It is a great story, one for all ages. But in all of my life, growing up in suburban Minnesota, the only time I ever encountered angels with wings, cloaked shepherds, and exotic wise men was at Christmas time, during Christmas pageant time.   This exotic tale about a baby and a manger has become very predictable and familiar, every year the same thing.

Our church capitalizes on that; we always have the best Christmas pageant around, in large part because of the super-Christmas Mistletoe family. The kindergartners are the animals, cows and sheep mostly, the first and second graders are the multitude of angels, the third and fourth graders are shepherds, the fifth and sixth graders take the other various parts; the wise men bearing unusual gifts, the stage hands, and the Angel Gabriel. Gabriel is a coveted part because he or she gets to shout "HARK." Now there is an underused word, but such a great word! Hark!

In our church pageant, the part of the Holy Family is always played by a real family—with a real baby. Over the years, I have played my assigned parts (including the year I was the half-time Jesus). I was an angel (sort of), a shepherd, and one year I even got to shout HARK!—my final appearance. Ivy covered her ears and everyone laughed. Participation in the church pageant was not optional in my family.

By the time I was in middle school, I figured out how to avoid the pageants and most of the extravagant Christmas preparations. I was really not interested in that fairytale, and besides, Mom and Ivy got so worked up about it. I convinced them that I was most helpful by staying out of their way. Until that fateful year I was a senior in high school, when everything changed.

All through middle school and high school, Ivy and I shared a job as nanny for the Forester family. Joe and Mary Forester lived only a few houses from us, and they had two cute kids, Sam and Emily. They were very involved in the community and in our church. Mom and Mary had their hands in every project at the Community Church. You know those in-everything kind of ladies. But one year was different. My easy-going part-time shared nanny job took on new significance. In April, Mary Forester was 8 months pregnant, when she was diagnosed with breast cancer. Little Max was born on May 12. Max was perfect, an unexpected gift to the family, and to all of us.

But immediately, Mary had to begin rigorous treatment for her cancer. Ivy and I took turns watching Sam and Emily after school and on weekends, while our mom helped with Max. We pitched in with errands and cleaning and anything the family needed. The Foresters became our summer job as well, as Mary's chemo treatments became more intense. It was a scary time. By late summer, Mary had lost all her hair and she had no energy to spare. Ivy was good at organizing and getting things done, but I was immobilized by this tragic situation. What I could do was hold and cuddle Max, and that became my mission and the greatest gift—to me. Max seemed to be the forgotten one, the one who came just as everything was thrown into chaos. Things were anything but normal for this new baby. He came at just the wrong time, or maybe just the right time. What I do know, is that he changed my life in a big way. Little Max was just what I needed, what the Forester family needed, and what we all needed then, and to this day. A baby born to teach us all how to love.

As fall approached, Sam started 4th grade and Emily 1st. Ivy and I began our senior year of high school. The needs of the Forester family were as great as ever, and we spent as much time with them as we could. They were now our family and we were invested in their struggles. Mary slowly regained some of her energy and she was determined to take on a few of her responsibilities again. By mid-October, the Christmas pageantry began, and Mary, Mom and Ivy were in it up to their eyeballs. They were director, choreographer, costume management team, and treat providers. I tried to ignore all of that stuff and go on with my normal routines.

But then it was decided that Joe and Mary and Max would be the Holy Family. I silently protested. It would be too much for Mary and they had enough on their plates already. How could they? What would that mean for Max? For me? But, ultimately they were the unanimous choice of the pageant committee. So, despite my best efforts, I got dragged back into the dreaded "Christmas Pageant"!

I did my part to get Sam and Emily to practices when needed. I spent time with them rehearsing their parts—shepherd shepherding and angel—well, looking angelic, I guess, (at least not looking like a Jedi Princess ready for battle). Max, well Max, I knew he would be okay if he felt he was secure and near the ones he loved most. For Mr. and Mrs. Forester, it was tough. Mary had finished her final chemo only weeks before, and she did not feel great. Joe had been strong throughout and he was the first one to accept this challenge and honor. I think that somehow he knew that this would be an important time for his family. And so it was; Sam a shepherd, and Emily an angel. Ivy would be a great angel coach. I was to have primary responsibility for Max before the show, making sure that he was fed and rested and changed. My mission was a contented, swaddled baby Jesus.

Pageant day came. I knew there would be some difficult moments as Mary prepared for her journey to Bethlehem. She decided not to wear her short curly wig, but to wrap her smooth head in a long beautiful scarf instead. Joe was a rock, and a great encouragement for all of us.

The time came and the narrator began the familiar story, "In those days a decree went out from Emperor Augustus that all the world should be registered." Then off to the right side of the chancel, the Children's choir began to sing, "Hark, the Herald Angels Sing." Angels appeared from everywhere.

"Joseph went from the town of Nazareth in Galilee to Judea, to the city of David called Bethlehem, because he was descended from the house and family of David. He went to be registered with Mary, to whom he was engaged and who was expecting a child." The Foresters entered from the left of the stage, Mary sitting sideways on the rolling donkey, very pregnant, while Joe walking calmly beside. I held Max as tightly as I could as we crouched behind the stable. "While they were there, the time came for her to deliver her child. And she gave birth to her firstborn son and wrapped him in swaddling clothes," (that was my cue to put Max gently into the straw-filled manger) "and she laid him in a manger because there was no room for them at the inn."

Max panicked as he looked around at the multitude of angels, and heard the approaching footsteps of the burlap-covered shepherds, even the two hovering adults with their head gear did not look familiar—he scrunched up his face, held his breath till he turned red, and was about to let out an ear-piercing scream. But just at that moment, the light crew got the spot going over the manger. The star was lit, and the angel said to Mary "Do not be afraid, Mary, for you have found favor with God." Mary grabbed Max out of the manger—her headscarf fell to the side, revealing the undisguised face and smooth head that Max recognized as Mom. As quickly as it came, the panic left baby Max and with a few choked whimpers under the light of the star, he gave Mary and Joseph a tender smile of relief and love. Sam and Emily had slowly inched closer and closer to the manger until finally, they surrounded the Holy Family for a big family bear hug. The audience cheered, I could finally breathe again, and the tears streamed down my face. Just then the Children's choir began to sing, "Away in a manger, no crib for a bed. The little Lord Jesus, lay down his sweet head. The stars in the sky look down where he lay, the Little Lord Jesus asleep on the hay," well maybe not sleeping, but certainly contented.

Do you get it? I think it was that moment when I finally got it. It is about love, love freely and abundantly given, but love that must be given away, whenever and wherever it is received. It's not about some list, or tallying up more good deeds than naughty ones. It's not about love that gets you something, but about love that persuades you that what you do with it is what is important—love given to one another.

Love has no power, unless and until it is given away. Love given is more powerful than fame or fortune or fear. Mary and Joe and Max taught me that, in that moment. The story of Jesus teaches us this for a lifetime. Let angels proclaim, let shepherds see stars, let wise men bring gifts, for this is the greatest story of our lives. And it is worthy to be celebrated again and again—every year, and for every generation.

Do not be afraid, for you have found favor with God. May your Christmas be richly blessed, as you give your love away—abundantly.

Luke 1:30
The angel said "Do not be afraid, Mary, for you have found favor with God."

48

I Heard The Bells on Christmas Eve

by S. Lindy Purdy

I love stories. I told this story to my friend Kris Krengel . . . that is really her name, and she asked me to share it with you. It's the story of our little town's "Bellegan-za." I guess I should start properly. My name is Andrea Belle, I was named after my two grandmothers—Andrea and Belle. Most people call me Belle. After I married my college sweetheart, Joe Peale, we moved to his hometown of Carillon, Minnesota, so he could join the law firm that his great grandfather Charles Edmond Peale started in 1923. Ten years ago, when Joe joined the firm, it became Peale, Peale and Peale, Attorneys-at-Law, or as Joe's little sister refers to them, Peale, Appeal and Repeal. Well, I guess I married into the right family, for now I am Belle Peale.

On December 24th of last year, our church, the First Community Church of Carillon celebrated its 100th birthday. The very first services were held on Christmas Eve, 1909 in the Carillon High School auditorium. Joe's great-great-grandparents were charter members of First Community, two of the 27 Carillon residents who gathered on that day to welcome the Christ Child, and to establish only the second church in town. Joe's great-great-grandfather, Edmond was the chairman of the building committee for the church, and the only thing he insisted on was that First Community have a proper bell tower. When the building was complete, the bell tower was dedicated to Edmond Grant and Sophie Adeline Peale.

Bells are part of the Peale's history. Edmond's heritage goes way back to a little town in England where hand bells originated. In those days, the bells were huge, and were hung high in a tower on the town square. Each bell was operated by a ringer, who pulled down on a rope to get the clapper to clang the side of the bell. From the town center, the bells could be heard throughout the town and into the nearby countryside. Doesn't that sound beautiful?

Well, it was beautiful for visitors and for country folk who came into town for the bell concerts on Sunday afternoons, but it was not so lovely for the town residents who had to listen to the grueling rehearsals that were held on Wednesday evenings and Saturday mornings. In fact, they became downright annoyed by the bells. The bells became so irritating that an anonymous resident wrote this poem to the Editor of the local newspaper.

> *Offenders of the human race*
> *Your bells are always ringing,*
> *We wish the ropes around your necks*
> *And you upon them swinging.*

Sometime, not too long after that poem appeared in the paper, and about the time the town council was prepared to vote for the removal of the bells, a clever fellow, Don Harmony, came up with the idea for "hand bells." With these smaller, portable bells, the ringers could do all their rehearsals inside. This part of my story is mostly true, and it is also true that PT Barnham is credited with introducing and promoting hand bells in this country.

With that history from Edmond's little town in England, you can imagine how important it was to the Peales that Carillon have a bell tower, and what better place than the new First Community Church. To this day, the bells of Carillon ring out twice a day to the community and beyond.

First Community got into hand bells early, too. In the 1960s the first set of Schulmerick hand bells were purchased with memorials gifts given in honor of Joe's great-grandmother, Catherine Peale. So, when I became a Peale, and a citizen of Carillon, becoming part of the First Community Church was not an option—it was an inheritance.

Ironically, my major in college was elementary education with an emphasis in music. While Joe was in law school, I got a job at a local church as the children's music director. That was my first experience ringing bells, and I was hooked. When we settled in Carillon, the first thing I did was join First Community's bell choir. Just imagine how excited Joe's family was to have a Belle in the family—who was also a "bell lover."

I somehow thought this would give me a bye on the family Christmas cookie baking frenzy. A no-cookie-baking-Christmas is my kind of Christmas.

Well, I am not the only one back home who is hooked on bells, it seems everyone at First Community is a little bell-crazy! We have a men's bell group—for fun they call themselves the "Men with Bells," and we have an awesome Concert Bell Choir that tours the Midwest every year. They even took their bells to Ireland two years ago. Neal Boardson directs the men and the Concert Bells, and I now direct the Children's Bell Choir. We have over forty kids from age ten to eighteen. The eight high school kids play in a Bell Ensemble at all the High School Choir concerts as well. We are quite a group of chimers when we're all in one place with our bells ringing.

Anyway, Carly Stovern, one of the bass bell players, was elected mayor of Carillon last year, and she had this grand idea that we would gather the whole town together on Christmas Eve morning for a "blow-out" of bells. This would honor our church's 100th anniversary, Carillon's Community Christmas Party, and of course, Jesus' birthday. The idea came in January, when the city council was setting its calendar for the coming year.

At first, the idea seemed underwhelming—there were so many other items that needed attention. But then in March, the "Men with Bells" won a prestigious talent competition at the University of Minnesota, and they were invited to ring from a float in the Aquatennial Parade in July. At the April meeting, the permit for the Christmas Eve Parade came before the council, and Carly's idea was reintroduced and this time it was greeted with great excitement. A Bell Extravaganza—"Belleganza." A motion passed unanimously. The first ever, Carillon Belleganza would be held at 10:00 a.m. on December 24th, in the center of town, right on the front lawn of the First Community Church of Carillon. How convenient, since First Community had the only carillon bell tower in town. First Community would be the sponsoring organization, but all residents of Carillon would be invited to take part.

A committee was formed, that is how things get done in our church. Rena Sailor was elected to chair the committee and she quickly organized her troops—choosing from the highly talented, task-oriented, enthusiastic folks in the community.

Right away, it was decided that invitations would be sent to all the residents of Carillon. This would be a community-wide event and Shirley volunteered to send out invitations to all the other churches—"ding-a-lings" from all corners of the community. The more bells the merrier!! After all, who would be the most likely to have the additional bells that would be needed for such an event. Judy volunteered to look into other kinds of bells and other ways that bells could be included in the Belleganza. Wouldn't it be great if every single person could ring out in some way? If you know Judy, you would know that nothing is impossible. It was pretty much a done deal that everyone would participate. Polly volunteered to organize a fundraiser to cover the modest costs that would be incurred in the promotion, and she would act as the accountant for the "Belleganza" as well. Sandy volunteered to work with the various bell choirs at our church, get the Chamber of Commerce involved, and see if the Leagaires singers and dancers would help with the choreography. The Board of Fellowship promised to have plenty of snacks on hand for meetings and rehearsals.

It was truly amazing how this group got off to such a lively start. When we told Pastor John about this event, he was nervous, very nervous. He knew what Christmas Eve was like. He urged us to consider holding this event on the 4th of July, or Memorial Day or maybe even on Valentine's Day, his favorite of all holidays—a "Belleganza" serenade for your sweetheart! Finally, he gave his blessing and promised to put it on his calendar.

As the planning for this event got rolling, it quickly became apparent that in addition to the largest ensemble of bells ever assembled in Carillon, this event had to include a celebration of the birth of Jesus. So it was decided that a "live" nativity would be part of the "Bellaganza." Autumn St. Chime was selected as the director, and a costume manager and choreographer were selected to assist her. I can brag a little here, because we have wonderful talent in the arts at First Community.

By early October, we were holding auditions for the major parts. Mary and Joseph, the Three Kings and the Angel Gabriel would be auditioned parts. The children's choirs from all the churches in town would be invited to be shepherds, and the older kids would handle the angels on a stick—that sounded weird, but we have these fabulous angels that are attached to long poles so they can fly around above the action.

Everyone in town would be invited to come to the manger as costumed animals, or bring an animal—stuffed animals preferred. The one requirement—everyone had to wear a bell, carry a bell or have a bell sewn into their costume.

Right after Thanksgiving, the details started to fall into place. The first priority was that everyone had a bell to ring at the appropriate time. Gabe, our personnel director, made staffs for all the shepherds with bells hanging from the crooks. The Citizen's Bank of Carillon donated 200 cow bells for all the animals and spectators at the "stable," and the Thimblebees made sure that all the hovering angels had jingle bells attached to the tips of their wings. Meanwhile the joint bell choir, under the direction of Neal Boardson, began to practice every Saturday morning. Even the singing choir would have a part, and they added two songs about bells to their Christmas repertoire.

The week before Christmas, Autumn called all the nativity participants together to rehearse their roles. 13-year-old Maggie was Mary—selected because of her angelic smile, and 12-year-old Ben was Joseph—selected maybe because he was the son of the mayor—but who really knows. The selection of the Angel Gabriel was a perfect choice—Charlie was the outgoing high school guy that every kid looked up to and wanted to fol-low—even to the church youth group. Charlie was also a good sport and strong enough to shoulder the giant, heavy angel wings that were part of Gabriel's garb. The Three Kings were actually two middle school girls and one guy, elegantly dressed in satin and gold, with tall ornate hats. It would be a challenge for these middle-school kids to stand still so their hats stayed upright on their heads. There would be twenty-seven shepherds, give or take a few, all with ringing staffs. (Maybe we should have thought that idea through a little more.) Rena found a beautiful, doll with a very life-like face at the summer rummage sale, and a very good decision was made to have the doll be the baby Jesus instead of a real newborn. Who knew what might happen, and besides, the temperatures are typically only in the 30s at that time of year.

The staging was perfect, but inconvenient for our buildings and ground crew, who had to make sure we were ready for Christmas Eve services later that day. The stable was placed right under the portico of the front steps of the church, and the hay-filled manger was front and center. Special risers and tables were assembled by the Trustees to accommodate more than 100 bell ringers. The circle drive up to the front door of the church was closed to cars and by 10:00 p.m. on Christmas Eve Eve, the stage was set.

On Christmas Eve morning, the participants were on the spot at 9:30 a.m. and the Carillon Bells in the bell tower started playing Christmas carols. The Board of Fellowship was there early to make sure that hot coffee and cider, and of course, Karen's homemade cookies were ready to go. By 9:50, the place was packed. The more than 100 ringers were ready. Mary, Joseph, baby Jesus, Gabriel, Casper, Melchior and Balthazar were in place, the angels were hovering, the shepherds were "keeping watch" (mostly watching the bells dangling from the crooks of their staffs, and also keeping watch for their parents in the gathering crowd). One of the littlest shepherds—Peter, quiet, gentle Peter, was so entranced with the baby Jesus, he dropped his staff and crept up the steps to the manger. He put his face right up to the baby's face, as if whispering something in his tiny ear.

The bells in the tower began to play "Away in the Manger," and as Mayor Carly stepped forward to offer a word of welcome, she looked down and saw an empty manger. At the same moment, as if prompted by her panicked expression, Mary and Joseph looked down at the manger, jumped back and looked frantically around the stable. The baby had disappeared before their eyes.

Right then, Pastor John, who was waiting to say the opening prayer, stepped forward to offer a word of comfort and assurance in the ensuing chaos.

Meanwhile, the director and her crew went to work searching the stable—no Jesus. The shepherds dispersed to their parent's for reassurance and the angel multitude took a pause from flying. Right then, Matt and Kelly Anderson noticed they were missing a child. They yelled for Peter, but Peter was nowhere to be seen. Peter is a special kid—he is such a sweet and sensitive boy, often seeing the world in a different way from his peers. But disappearing, that was just not like Peter.

An announcement was made to the gathered crowd, and immediately the entire town was searching for little Peter. A perimeter was defined and watchers were set up to make sure that no one would be able to wander away. The crowd stayed alert and on edge. Teams were sent to scour the grounds.

Gabriel, Charlie in real life, had a hunch. Peter was his neighbor and Charlie spent time each week with Peter. He sensed that Peter might have found a quiet spot away from the crowd. He went inside the church and into the narthex, where he saw that the door to the bell tower was open. He listened carefully, and heard a muffled voice coming down from the spiral stairs. He began to climb the thirty two steps of the tower and as he rounded the last turn, there he saw Peter, gently rocking the swaddled baby Jesus, singing to him "the stars in the sky look down where he lay, the little Lord Jesus asleep in the hay." As Charlie drew nearer—Peter said, "Shhhh . . . Jesus is sleeping, he likes the bells." That made it unanimous for sure—everyone in Carillon that day was a "bell fan."

As Charlie and Peter came back down, Peter was still clutching the baby Jesus. As the door opened, he ran into the arms of his grateful and relieved parents Matt and Kelly.

The bells in the tower began to play "I heard the bells on Christmas Eve." That was the cue that the "Bellaganza" was to begin. Everyone scurried back into place.

Peter would not loosen his grip on Jesus; he was hanging onto the Christ Child as if his life depended on it. So Charlie calmly walked over and took Peter's hand, and together they walked forward and sat on the front steps of the church, right next to the manger. Charlie held Peter and Peter held the precious baby. Right at 10:00 a.m., the bells in the bell tower stopped, and the show went on. The bell ringers began to ring, and the crowd stood in awe. As the angels took flight over the Holy Family, the first flakes of snow began to fall. Song after song, each more beautiful than the one before, rang out over the town of Carillon. When the concert was nearly over, all the people were invited to ring their bells together as they sang "Jingle Bells." By this time, the whole town was into it. The Holy Family led the singing, Peter and baby Jesus were hoisted up on to Charlie's shoulders, and Peter was grinning from ear to ear.

Then came the finale, everyone joined together in one last song—a song of sending, a song of blessing, voices and bells and children's glee all together. "Joy to the world the Lord has come, let earth receive her king. Let every heart, prepare him room, and heaven and nature sing, and heaven and nature ring, and heaven, heaven and nature sing."

Well, it was quite an anniversary celebration for First Community Church. We heard the bells on Christmas Eve. If you should hear any bells this year, let it remind you of the Christ child, God with us, the baby we celebrate at Christmas time. And, like Peter, never loosen your grip on Jesus. Hang on for dear life, hang on as if your life depends on it—because it does.

John 1:14
And the Word became flesh and lived among us, and we have seen his glory, the glory as of a father's only son, full of grace and truth.

LEFT HANGING

by S. Lindy Purdy

My name is Connie Frasier and it is a beautiful, white December morning. It is the perfect setting for telling you an amazing Christmas story. I am pretty sure that you will all be able to see yourselves somewhere in this story, especially you sentimental types.

Before I begin, I must share a few confessions with you. First, I cannot travel anywhere, even to a different part of town and not set my eyes on alert for a new and interesting Christmas ornament. I cannot pass the ornament displays at any store without checking them out. My second confession is that if I see an ornament that is interesting, adorable, creative, or reminds me of someone, I cannot pass it up. My third confession is that I love to make Christmas ornaments, and I have been doing it for more than 40 years. And my fourth confession is that I can't seem to part with any of these ornaments. Wow, four confessions in one day.

Now, imagine my basement storage room in the summer. There, along the wall, are seventeen jumbo plastic bins, all neatly labeled, "Christmas Ornaments." And that is after I gave each of my kids two bins of ornaments I had collected for them over the years.

This story takes place two years ago, when for the first time ever, I broke down and purchased an artificial tree. So actually, my story begins back in August, at the church rummage sale. On my way into the church, I saw the most realistic fake Christmas trees standing right near the entrance. One tree especially caught my attention as I made my way to the "Collectibles" department. It was just beautiful, so tall and full. It had lots of branches for my hundreds of ornaments.

I found many treasures that day, but on the way out to my car, the synthetic Christmas tree caught my eye again. I just couldn't resist, so I found one of the Boy Scouts to help me disassemble and pack up the tree and get it into my car. When I got home, I carefully slid it behind some boxes in the corner of my garage, so my husband would not notice another huge rummage sale purchase.

As Thanksgiving approached, and I began to think about my annual tree decorating ritual, I remembered my impulsive purchase. I felt a little sad about not having a real tree, pine scent and all, but I would get two live tabletop trees to use as centerpieces in the dining room.

My granddaughter Sophie and I have a tradition of decorating the Christmas tree on the Saturday after Thanksgiving. So, after the Thanksgiving dishes were washed, the Indian corn, gourds and pumpkins removed from the table, the Pilgrim diorama put into storage, the seventeen large plastic bins were carried up from the basement. This is a job that is required of anyone not involved in Thanksgiving kitchen clean-up. My son brought the box with the "new," recycled, rummage Christmas tree from the garage and set it in the middle of the living room. I had some second thoughts about a "second-hand" plastic tree. "What was I thinking?" "What would Sophie think?" Oh well, I could always go get a "real" tree if it was too bad.

That Saturday, Sophie arrived at 9:00 a.m. and we couldn't wait to get started. We opened the box labeled "Special Ornaments" first. I knew the treasures in there would get us in the mood for the task ahead.

Sophie took out the first ornament; it was the gold Santa sleigh with a photo of my kids riding atop Santa's toys—they were about four and six. Sophie stared at her six year old dad with delight and amusement—she would be six next June. Then my eye caught a clothespin reindeer, the ornament we made as family gifts over twenty years ago. I remember we all sat around the kitchen table gluing eyes and antlers and tails, and painting smiles and hoofs on each of those Christmas creatures. Then Sophie dragged out the macaroni wreath that my daughter made in first grade —only a few elbow-macs missing. How could I part with that? Sophie immediately wanted to make one of her own, but that would have to wait. Then there was the hammer, an empty thread spool painted brown, attached to a dowel and hanging from a piece of red yarn.

Left Hanging

My son brought it home from school the year the second graders sang "All Over This Land" for the holiday concert.

It's the hammer of justice,
It's the bell of freedom,
It's a song about love between my brothers and my sisters,
Alllllll over this laaaaand. Ooooooo

A real Christmas classic?

Oh, and the five golden rings (gold plastic curtain hooks) on a red and green ribbon; the gift of the fifth day of Christmas. That was from a Secret Santa exchange many years ago. My husband was the recipient of the gifts of all twelve days. He especially liked the nine ladies dancing. Do you have any idea how many Drummers, Pipers, Lords and Ladies, Birds, Hens, Doves and Partridges that is? I had to do the math—364 in total.

Next we took out the precious popsicle-stick angels, each bearing one of my children's sweet faces. A few years ago, one of the angels escaped, never to be found. It was on a special mission I hoped. My son carefully recreated it for me for Christmas the next year. It is one of my all-time favorite gifts.

In that special box are homemade ornaments: cross-stitched, painted, sewn, colored, glued, and assembled. There are ornaments with photos of the kids made from their school pictures—from pre-school to present. Many of these ornaments have had an adventure along the way—like the crescent moon ornament that I HAD to have for my daughter—symbolic of her sorority, Gamma Phi. My husband and I were on a canal tour in Bruge, Belgium and I spied a beautiful crystal blue crescent moon in the window of a shop as we floated by. It took us almost two hours to find our way back to that shop by foot, only to find that it had a slight flaw, and it was the only one. Flaw and all, it came home with us and made its way to the "Special Ornaments" box. Then there was the year that we got our one and only dog—a Bichon Frise named Marquis—the Marquis du Fluff. I must have gone to 20 ornament shops, but no little white fluffy dog. So I saved some of Marquis' fluffy fur when he was at the doggy salon, and sent it to a shop in Ely, MN where they specialized in creating furry animal ornaments from real animal fur. This year, 24 years later, Marquis looked a little disheveled, but Sophie cuddled him anyway.

61

And the heart, the heart makes me cry every time. The Christmas after my dad died, I found a heart shaped ornament with a lid that opened. I asked everyone to write down a word that described my dad, and I loaded all the words into the heart ornament—"adventurous," "one of a kind," "generous," "clever," "entertaining," "fun and funny," "erudite," "obstreperous." He was all of those things—captured in that special ornament.

What a walk down memory lane! As we laid all the "special" ornaments out on the coffee table, I decided it was time—time to confront the "fake tree." I carefully opened the box; the instructions were long gone. What to do first? There was a stand and a thick, green pole; that must be the first step. So I set the trunk into the stand and began to arrange the greenery on the floor, sorting by size. Sophie thought it was a puzzle, and she quickly started to help arrange the boughs.

We started attaching the larger branches around the bottom of the tree, then up to the next layer and the next. Pretty soon the tree began to take shape. It was not bad. Unless my nose was playing tricks on me, it even smelled slightly like pine. The final branch, almost like a small tree itself, set right into the top of the trunk, completing the tree. It was really quite stunning. We had to walk around it a few times, to make sure it was showing its best side. It didn't have a best side.

As I examined the tree, checking to make sure each branch was just right, I saw something wedged in the tree about shoulder height. It was almost completely hidden by the thick branches. I reached in and felt it. It was securely attached to a branch. It felt like a velvet jewelry box, about an inch or an inch and a half square, tied to a branch with a silver ribbon. As I felt around it, I found the loose end that set it free, then carefully extracted it from its hiding place. This had been someone else's tree, and this was someone else's special ornament. It seemed almost too dear to open. I set it aside, looking for any other clues, any other ornaments or treasures left by a previous owner. The only other things I found were a bent ornament hook and a few strands of tinsel.

I knew I would have to open that box or it would drive me crazy. I had to know what was inside. Sophie was jumping up and down with excitement. She immediately began imagining the contents—a secret treasure, a $100 dollar bill, a diamond ring.

Left Hanging

It was probably nothing; a forgotten ornament, left hanging on a tree, past its season. That happened more than once to us—maybe that is what happened to the popsicle stick angel.

Curiosity got the best of us. We took the velvet box and gave it a little shake; no rattle, no jingle, no sound, no clue. Then we opened the little box and found that it contained a rolled up note—tied with a matching silver ribbon.

We carefully unrolled the little scroll. Sophie deciphered many of the words, and as the message became clear, tears formed in my eyes. I guess it was the sentimentality of the day, but the message was so sweet, and so mysterious.

Now what was I to do? This message was obviously not for me, not for anyone I knew. It was a message that got hung up on a beautiful Christmas tree that belonged to someone else, and I had no idea who that was. Did this message ever make it to the intended person? Did Joe ever get a response back? Now I was worried. What if somehow, this message, carefully hidden in the branches of a recycled Christmas tree, was never found? I wondered how this ornament was left hanging, and whether Joe was left hanging as well.

I read the note out loud.

Dear Mary,
You are the best Christmas present I could ever dream of. I have been silly and selfish, but I believe with my whole heart that we are destined to be together. I hope that when you find this box tied to the bough of your Christmas tree, you will also know that I am ready to tie my life to yours. This key is for Postal Box 347, where you will find tickets and itinerary to join me and my family in Montana to celebrate the New Year. If I do not see you on New Year's Day, I will know that you have moved on and I will not try to contact you again. With all my love, Joe.

Sophie was the first to see it. Taped inside the top of the box was a silver key, with the number 347 punched into the metal. Sophie and I looked at each other in amazement. What should we do? Continue decorating our Christmas tree? When we now knew a secret that could change the lives of two people? The velvet box was just too compelling. We had to find that postal box—but which post office? By now it was well after closing time at any post office, too late to start investigating. I was guessing that the post office in question was not too far from Wayzata, since that is where the Christmas tree ended up. But that would have to wait 'til Monday.

Besides, I was committed to help with the Children's Christmas Pageant and the Women's Fellowship bake sale tomorrow and I hadn't started baking a thing. Sophie and I had only started decorating the tree, but the time had flown and the rest of the tree would have to wait for another day.

I took Sophie home, picked up the ingredients I needed to make our family's favorite sugar cookies and headed home for an evening of baking. But the mysterious ornament was never far from my mind. My husband George had arrived home and was amazed at the tree, the tree that he did not have to wrestle into the stand, the tree that he did not have to twist and turn to find a "good" side. I think he liked it. At least he said he did.

I told him about the mysterious velvet box we found, and he chuckled at what a great advertising gimmick that was. "Included with every tree, a clue to an unsolved romantic mystery." He thought it was cute that Sophie was there to watch me find it, but I don't think he gave it another thought. Of course, I could think of nothing but the velvet box. Between batches of cookies, I did an internet search of all the post offices within a 50-mile radius of Wayzata. There were 37 with postal boxes for rent. I also looked in the church directory for families with a "Mary." There were several—too many to actually be helpful.

The next morning was hectic. I glanced at the tree, thinking it was still quite striking. Maybe it was a good decision after all. Meanwhile, my daughter-in-law called and told me that Sophie could not stop talking about the hidden treasure box. She wanted to know if I would bring it to the pageant so she could show it to her friends. Sophie was one of the angels. Then I remembered that I promised I would hem her white crepe skirt and sew the elastic on the angel wings.

The morning was a blur, but I did remember to put the velvet box and its message in my purse before I ran out the door. I got to church just in time to unload the cookies, get hot water started for the cocoa, and meet Sophie as she came bursting through the door. She grabbed her skirt and wings and was off to the music room to practice her songs. The kindergartners and first graders were the angels and they were singing three songs. We had all been asked to listen to Sophie sing her part, "Away in a Manger" for many weeks. We were all pretty exciting when the day of the pagent arrived. For a while, I forgot to think about the velvet box with the key inside.

My husband George had been at church all morning. He volunteered every year to be part of the set crew. The high school gang, under the direction of the amazing and handsome Joe Browning, had the set design and building duties every year. The sets were wonderful, and a little creative in some of their Bethlehem motifs. Like the "Wise Guys Café" and the "Dancin' with the Star" billboards.

Crowds were beginning to gather; the kind of crowds carrying cameras and hurrying for a front row seat. It had to be the pageant, nobody ever hurried to the front row in church on Sundays. I was helping the kids line up in the hall as they waited for their entrance. Sophie walked by and saw me and asked if I had the special box. She wanted so badly to see it, so I took it from my purse. She grabbed it from my hand. The time came for the host of heavenly angels to take their position over the fields of Bethlehem, and Sophie took off in a rush.

As the last spectators were arriving, Pastor John strolled onto the chancel for his warm welcome. He loves this event, he loves kids, and he loves the stage. The pageant began. Mary and Joseph walked to the set by way of the center aisle and took their place behind the wooden manger. The live baby Jesus entered stage right by way of his real mother's arms and was placed in the manger. The baby Jesus was already seven months old and would have nothing to do with lying down in the manger, so he sat up. He was mesmerized by the scene, looking all around, from one shepherd to another.

The angels began to sing "Away in a Manger," and I could see Sophie and her friend Lily edging closer and closer to the baby Jesus. By the time the song was finished, they were patting baby Jesus on the head, much to Jesus' delight.

In marched the Kings—there were about twelve of them. You know it never says in the Bible how many kings there were. Twelve assorted Kings, all bearing gifts, moved around the manger singing "We Three Kings of Orient are, Bearing gifts we travel so far." All of the Kings were trying to get the baby Jesus to look at, or grab the gifts they held out. Sophie was still very close to the manger, and she held out her gift as well—the mysterious velvet box. For some reason, Jesus liked that gift best. He grabbed at it and finally took it from Sophie's hand. It went right to his mouth. Sophie proudly and loudly announced that the box had a key inside with a secret love letter and that her grandmother found it on their new Christmas tree. The boys were unimpressed, but the girls wanted to see inside. Baby Jesus just wanted to chew on the soft box.

Standing nearby, ready to avert any set disasters, was Joe Browning. I was standing next to him because I was in charge of getting the kindergartners and first graders off stage, so I witnessed Joe's reaction as he listened intently to Sophie's story. I could see the confusion on his face.

As soon as the pageant ended and the last kids were happily reunited with their parents, he rushed out from behind the stage. He grabbed me by the elbow and blurted, "How did Sophie get that box? If Sophie had it, maybe Mary never found it on the tree. I put it in plain site, right at the front, tied with a silver bow. Why did you have that tree? What did the note say? You must get it and show it to me. It might be the same box I tied to the branches last year!" I finally broke his constant questioning long enough to say, "Let's go find Sophie and you can see for yourself."

We rushed out to the community room into a mob of excited kids and adoring parents and grandparents. After looking for a while, we spotted Sophie and her parents not too far from the cocoa machine. As we approached, Sophie was full of hugs and kisses. She did not have the velvet box. "Sophie, where is it?" "I guess I left it with baby Jesus." Joe and I rushed to the manger on the set. The high school kids were just taking all the stage props to the undercroft, but we caught up to Nathan as he was carrying the manger out of the sanctuary. Joe raked through the straw with his fingers, and came up with the treasure he was looking for. "Mrs. Frasier, what should I do? If she didn't get this, she must have thought I never wanted to see her again."

"The last thing I said is that I needed a time out. I haven't even seen her around lately and we always seemed to be in the same place at the same time—before. She has probably moved on. I may never see her again." "Joe, isn't Mary the girl you used to hang out with here at church?" "Well, yes." "Weren't she and her family members here?" "Yes." "Let's go look at the database and see if they are still around this area."

We rushed to the office and found one of the office personnel. She looked up the Rudolph family and discovered that they moved in early March to Costa Rica. Thus, the rummage Christmas tree. Their current phone number was listed. Joe immediately grabbed his cell phone and dialed. A man answered and Joe began to explain the reason for his call.

Mr. Rudolph listened patiently and said only, "What a year this must have been for both of you. Mary is living in Stillwater where she is teaching third grade. I think you need to talk to her." Mr. Rudolph gave Joe her phone number and that next call was made.

Do you think this story has a happy ending? I probably would not be here today if it didn't. Mary and Joe found each other again and the year that each of them spent doubting and wondering, made their reunion all the sweeter. They were married right here last summer, Mary Elizabeth Rudolph and Joseph John Browning became Mr. and Mrs. Mary and Joseph Browning, and they invited Jesus to be present at the ceremony.

After all, it was the gift given to Jesus that revealed the love that was lost, and Jesus who readily acknowledged their symbol of love at the pageant with such delight. That Jesus (Sam Carpenter) was now almost two years old, and Mary and Joe wanted him to be at their wedding. On the day of the wedding, Nathan brought the manger to the front of the church, and Sophie hid a small velvet box tied with silver ribbon in the straw.

In the velvet box were the rings that they gave to each other as an outward symbol of their inward love, and the unending symbols of God's love for each of them. Mary and Joseph invited Jesus to be part of their marriage, for they knew that it was only with Jesus at the center, that their marriage would be safe to grow freely and flourish for all the years to come.

What do you think that Mary and Joseph of Bethlehem would say to you today if they were here? Do not be afraid, for you have found favor with God? Be ready for the unexpected. The Mary of old certainly didn't expect to give birth to the Messiah. When the angel Gabriel came to Mary, "she was much perplexed by his words and pondered what sort of greeting this might be." (Luke 1:29) But she said, "Here I am, the servant of the Lord; let it be with me according to your word." (Luke 1:37) Maybe they would tell us, "Nothing will be impossible with God."

The Joseph of old was not about to be disgraced or to disgrace Mary. He did the unexpected, "he did as the angel of the Lord commanded him; he took Mary as his wife." (Matthew 1:24) And "Mary treasured all these words and pondered them in her heart." (Luke 2:19)

What would Mary and Joseph Browning say? I think they would tell us all to look for the unexpected in our own lives. Do not be afraid to wait, ponder the moments of joy, and do not let anything be left hanging on your Christmas tree. Merry Christmas!

AWAY IN A KENNEL

by S. Lindy Purdy

Sometimes they call me the storyteller. It seems my life is a series of stories. Sometimes a story begins, stalls out for many years, and then begins again. It does not even seem like a story I guess, until I can look back over all the chapters. I am Midge Thorson and the story that I want to tell started 25 years ago. That is where it begins, so I am taking you back to my high school years.

I first met Janie the fall of my junior year in high school. She was quiet, a good student. At first we hardly noticed her. She slipped in, hardly making a ripple. Her last name was Thompson—s-o-n, so we got her last name confused with the Petersons, Larsons, and Andersons. But in my homeroom, she sat near me—alphabetical you know—Thompson, Thorson.

I noticed sometime in November, she was gone for a while, long enough so everyone was asking, "Where is that girl Janie, you know the one with the blonde curly hair? Isn't she in your homeroom, Midge?" No one really knew much about her. She must have been gone two or three months, then one day she was back. She didn't speak about her absence, so we were left to wonder.

Later that spring, our science teacher, Mrs. Kollmeyer, asked for volunteers to help with a project. She and her husband had just become certified trainers for companion dogs. [Canine Companions for Independence (CCI) is a non-profit organization that enhances the lives of people with disabilities by providing highly trained assistance dogs.]

Mrs. Kollmeyer was asking for volunteers to work with two new puppies they had adopted for training. My hand shot up into the air so fast, I didn't even realize what I was doing—and so did Janie's. Before I had even processed the possibilities, I heard "Midge and Janie, that would be great. Let's talk after class."

Midge and Janie—we became a team. A puppy training team. From that day on, we were partners, spending countless hours together and eventually we became friends, the best of best friends. Over the next year, it was Midge and Janie, Oscar and Emmy. Oscar was Emmy's puppy brother, and they were adorable and playful and messy, and sometimes inconvenient. Mr. and Mrs. Kollmeyer did the intense training, but Janie and I were part of the team to provide variety and fun.

We took the dogs after school for two days a week, and for five hours on Saturdays. During summer break, we had them fifteen hours a week. Janie was really good at this. She had patience, and a way about her that made it seem like Oscar and Emmy understood every word she was saying. I was better at running and throwing a ball with them, but all Janie had to do was say "come," and they stopped what they were doing and sat right in front of her.

Well, it was a great experience—until February 23rd. That was the day that Oscar and Emmy graduated. They did it! We did it! They were ready to be placed with the companions they were trained to guide. It was so hard to say goodbye. We were not even allowed to know who their new owners were. Their absence created a big hole in my life. The emptiness felt even bigger when Janie and I saw each other, so we began to drift apart.

We would be graduating in a few months, and I was headed off to the University of Colorado, and Janie was headed down to some small school in Kentucky where her grandfather had been on the faculty. I know she had talked often about becoming a veterinarian, and I thought that was the perfect fit for her. I had no idea what I would study, I just loved the mountains.

I lasted a year in Colorado, then settled back home to finish my degree in Botany, hoping I could one day work at the arboretum near my home. Three years later I did finish my degree and get a part-time job working at the Minnesota Landscape Arboretum. I also got married and had two kids.

A few years after college, I ran into Janie at an animal adoption day for the Humane

Society. She had dropped out of school for a few years, but was in the process of applying to vet schools. We talked for a few minutes, mostly about the time we spent with Oscar and Emmy, and how they had influenced our lives in such amazing ways. We promised to stay in touch and find ways to share our lives. But you know how it is when you have a baby, the only people you stay in touch with are the pediatrician and the babysitter. Life is good, but time is always in short supply.

Now that you know a little of the background, I must tell you the most amazing story. It happened four years ago at Christmas time. The shopping was done, the stockings were hung, the pageants were history. It has become a tradition for my parents to invite our kids to their house the night before Christmas Eve. The idea was that they would help their grandparents wrap gifts and get ready for Christmas. But I knew it was really so that Mark and I could have a peaceful night before the chaos ensued. Four years ago, our kids were eight and ten, and they were hyper-excited for Christmas—emphasis on the hyper.

I made reservations for the night at the Hounds and Hills Bed and Breakfast in Stillwater, about an hour from our home. It had only been open for a year or two, and some friends gave it a glowing recommendation. We dropped the kids and the dogs off with their grandparents and off we went.

It was about 3:00 in the afternoon when we entered the town of Stillwater. A few big, fluffy snowflakes were falling. Perfect! We drove up to the Hounds and Hills B & B, an Old Victorian House restored and lovingly decorated for Christmas. Next to it was a low building with arched windows that might have been a carriage house at one time, or an elaborate outbuilding for the estate. Over the door was a sign, "Welcome to our Four-Legged Guests." These two guest houses were side-by-side, nestled in the hills on the west side of town.

We parked in the circle drive that led to the front door of the Victorian house. We were greeted with a needle-point sign that read, "Welcome Guests, You are Family Here." We walked into a beautiful room that looked like a parlor, straight from the early 1900s. A fire was smoldering in the fireplace and ginger cookies and hot apple cider were waiting for guests to arrive. I immediately noticed a young girl, sitting at a table wrapping gifts, and at her feet was a golden retriever. The dog was wearing a vest—a canine companion vest. I moved to get nearer to the dog, and the young girl said, "Her name is Sammy." I looked longingly at Sammy, as the young girl left her chair and brought the guest book to my husband. She handed us a key, and we found our room on the second floor.

Mark was eager to keep moving, so we stashed our overnight bags and went back downstairs. Sammy and the young girl were gone, and an older gentleman was sitting behind the table with his newspaper. He greeted us, "Good afternoon Mr. and Mrs. Morgan, I hope your room suits you. I'm Phillip, and I oversee this place. Let me know if there is anything you need."

We were on our way to town, so we hopped in the car for a five minute drive into downtown Stillwater. The town was busy, and cheerful. It was Christmas Eve Eve and the merchants were busy welcoming and enticing last-minute shoppers with music and treats and big "SALE" signs. Mark and I walked along the river walk, as snow continued to fall. It was beginning to get dark and the lights of the city were coming on. We had dinner reservations at 6:00 and after that a local radio station was running a light show on the lift-bridge.

It was a glorious evening, almost like a fairyland. All the while, the snow kept coming, and as we walked back to our car, we noticed there was a significant accumulation. Our car looked like a mound of snow on the street. We scooped and scraped the snow off, and started back for the Hounds and Hills. It was slow going, the streets were drifted with snow, and as we came near our home-away-from-home, we could see the Victorian house decorated with white lights outlining every architectural feature, and the colorfully lighted arches of the carriage house. We were sure glad we had an early start, or we might never have made it to Stillwater that day.

We stomped the snow from our feet as we entered the parlor. Phillip was waiting, glad for our safe return. All his guests were accounted for, except one couple—Joe and Mary Eastman. He was visibly anxious about their delayed arrival. He invited us to sit for tea, and we gladly accepted. We asked him about the B & B, and he offered a brief history. "It belongs to my niece, Jane. She is almost never here, so I pretty much run it, at least this part. The Animal Inn over there is Jane's passion." I asked him about the young girl who met us when we first arrived. Phillip said, "Oh, that is Chrissy, she lives here now. Did she say anything? Chrissy is autistic, sometimes she isn't very friendly." We assured Phillip that she was fine, that she had told us the dog's name is Sammy. "It that her dog?" I asked. "Yes, well yes it is. Sammy is Jane's baby, but Sammy is becoming Chrissy's companion more and more each day."

Over tea, we found out that Jane is a vet in town. And she also runs the Pet Inn next door which is a licensed dog breeding and training center for companion dogs, as well as a boarding kennel for dogs when their owners are out of town. Phillip proudly announced that both inns were full for the night, and six new puppies were born just yesterday. I couldn't wait to see them.

I asked Phillip to tell me more about his niece. He said, "Well she is about your age, she's ambitious and generous and she adores dogs. She had rough start in life, but I think she has found her home and her passion here." I asked him more about Jane. "She lives in an apartment on the back side of the Animal Inn, and Chrissy lives with her. Chrissy was abandoned as a pre-schooler, in a town where Jane worked for a while. She certainly has blossomed here at the Pet Inn—she's Jane's shadow and assistant."

I was full of questions. Phillip was distracted, but I managed to find out that Jane spent some time in Minnesota during her high school years, but not much more. It was getting late, and Mark and I were ready to retire for the evening, when the doorbell began to ring repeatedly. Phillip ran for the door and found a young man frantic for help. "My wife, my wife—come, come." Phillip seemed frozen, like he did not know what to do, so I urged Mark to go with the man and I followed.

The snow was still coming and the drifts were as high as I had ever seen them. We ran out to the road, following the insistent visitor. We made it to the van and the young man said, "My wife is in labor and we need help." Mark and I were speechless. We started to open the side door, when an arm pushed us out of the way and took over. "You—get in the back seat and be ready to lift her head, you hold her feet up", then she turned to the young man and said, "grab her around the hips and pull her gently toward the door." We all did as she instructed, mostly because we could not imagine doing anything else. Phillip joined us and slowly she was pulled from the van.

In a mass, we slowly moved her toward the house. With Chrissy and Sammy right at her side, the woman in command directed us not to the Hounds and Hills, but to the Animal Inn. We were in snow that was over our knees, and the young woman we were carrying was in distress.

We became an instant team. We moved together following the calm and insistent instructions of our leader and finally we were at the back door of the Animal Inn. The door opened and we were instructed to place the woman on a large table. Chrissy was there in an instant with blankets and cushions. Confidently, our guide took over and we all found ourselves beholding a miracle.

On a snowy night, in an animal inn, we witnessed the birth of a beautiful baby girl. Her parents were ecstatic, the day-old puppies gathered around and crooned a lovely tune. Born this night in the city of Stillwater, a beautiful baby girl, to proud parents, Mary and Joseph, who were relieved and grateful. Baby girl Eastman arrived a little early, but at just the right time. She and those brand new puppies sang that night, and we, as bystanders were visibly moved. In a deep dark winter night, we witnessed a miracle, a baby born in a kennel.

Sammy settled right next to Chrissy, giving her the confidence to lead us in a carol. Two-legged and Four-legged creatures began to sing:

> *Away in a kennel, no crib for her bed,*
> *Baby girl Eastman lay down her sweet head,*
> *The snow in the sky cushioned her way,*
> *A miracle baby, now sleeping away.*

With everyone's help, the Eastman family settled into their room at the Hounds and Hills. Chrissy pulled out the bottom drawer of the armoire and padded it with a pillow. The baby was safe, and settled into an old T-shirt when we all finally went to our rooms. There was not much sleep that night.

At breakfast, we sat with Jane as Phillip prepared a simple breakfast. The sun and the snow plows were working hard, as we sat in the stillness of the morning and remembered our shared past and our new beginning. Jane was indeed Janie, the shy girl from my high school class, who volunteered as quickly as I did to be a nanny to Oscar and Emmy, companion dogs in training.

Janie was finally home—home in the most settled, peaceful, hopeful ways she had ever known. She had achieved her dream, and was helping so many others make their dreams come true. That year, we shared a Christmas miracle, and our lives will never be the same. By the way, my friend Janie and I have had a miraculous friendship over these last years. And every year about Christmas time, we get a photo of Gloria Eastman, our little Christmas baby.

> My wish for each of you this Christmas is that you will be
> able to experience once again the miracle of new life and
> of old friendships.

Luke 2:6-7
While they were there, the time came for her to deliver her child. And she gave birth to her firstborn son and wrapped him in bands of cloth, and laid him in a manger, because there was no place for them in the inn.

The story that I am about to tell you is different from others I have written. The whole premise of this story, and many of the details that are part of the story, are based on a true story. It might be called historical fiction.

And so I offer this story, entitled "V-Mail Courtship"
in memory of a dear woman in my congregation.

A number of years ago, when I visited her, she shared a box of letters with me. From them I have drawn my inspiration. The setting, the newspaper column and all of the V-mails are quotes from very real and precious letters (only a small number of which are contained in this story).

V-MAIL COURTSHIP

by S. Lindy Purdy

I am Jenny Standa and I am so glad to be able to tell you this wonderful story about my mother, Gloria. Gloria Meredith Shulstad was born on December 21,1920 in Stanley, Wisconsin, which is not too far from Eau Claire. She had two older brothers, so you can only imagine how spoiled she was. Her dad moved the family to Hopkins, Minnesota when my mom was seven and she lived there until after she graduated from Hopkins High School in 1938. In 1940, she graduated from the Minneapolis School of Business. It is so strange to think of my mom as a school girl, but I have seen evidence that she was, and she was pretty cute. I think I am more embarrassed looking at her High School yearbook than I am my own.

When I was growing up, Mom didn't talk much about those early years. I got the feeling that she held these memories close, pondering them in her heart. She seemed contented to care for the house and garden and my brother, Jim and me. But in 2006, a year before my dad died, we all went on a cruise—a 60th anniversary cruise in the Caribbean. It was my brother and his three kids, Kurt and I, our two daughters, and my mom's brother Edwin. One night we went up to the deck after dinner, just the four of us, Mom and Dad and Jim and I. It was a beautiful night and my dad suddenly brought up a long-held memory. I think it caught him by surprise. It was the memory of his only other experience on a ship, some 70 years ago.

My dad was an Army man, 34th Infantry Division, and it was a long ago voyage that took him from New York, across the Atlantic, into the European theater of World War Two. He spoke of that night years ago, saying, "I remember that cruise, it was in the dead of winter and the 400 other passengers were seasick and scared young men just like me—trying to be brave." Then my dad marveled at the way this big cruise ship felt so stable and steady, unlike the one that tossed and turned on the waves of the Atlantic so many years ago. I couldn't believe that I had never heard about that cruise before, or much about the war either. There had always been a photo of that handsome young soldier with his bride on the bookcase of our living room. Now I had lots of questions.

But all I found out that night, was that my dad would rather leave his memories of war in the past. I never was able to talk to him about his early life experiences, and after he died, my mom was too sad to talk about it.

Then three years ago, we moved my mom to assisted living and my brother and I began to clean out her house. We found an old trunk stashed in the back of a closet. My mom wanted to keep it with her, so we took it to her new apartment. She was not eager to share its contents, but as we were moving it, I caught a glimpse of what looked like my dad's old Army uniform inside. It was almost a year later, on a Sunday afternoon right before Christmas, that mom took the box out of that old trunk. She was finally ready to share her remarkable love story with me.

The box was tied with a pink ribbon, and inside were neatly organized bundles of letters. Lots of letters. Mom told me that when she finished business school, she went to work for a small chemical company as the secretary to the President. But when the war in Europe was heating up, she and most of her girlfriends went to work at the ordinance plant in New Brighton making ammunition.

Then in April of 1941, an interesting appeal appeared in Cedric Adam's column, "This

V-Mail Courtship

Corner" in the Minneapolis Star newspaper. She had the clipping and I read it. Charles Lynch, Minnesota lad now down at Camp Claiborne, Louisianna, wrote to Cedric Adams:

Correspondence Sweethearts Wanted:
I know that shape of yours isn't exactly suited to running around
without clothes on it shooting arrows, but won't you act as Cupid for us soldier boys
and line up some Minnesota girls with whom we might correspond?
There are plenty of fellows here who would like to develop a correspondence
with girls back home. It would help relieve our homesickness,
as well as, aid in passing our spare time.

Cedric responded:

Indeed we'll help.
So, girls, if you want to start a correspondence
with a Minnesota soldier now in camp, send your first letters to 'This Corner.'
Give your name, age, address and something about yourself.
We'll forward the letters to Private Lynch and he will pass them out to boys your ages
at camp and you're then on the road to helping our defense program.

Miss Gloria Meredith Shulstad wrote the next day.
I read that first letter.

April 23, 1941
Dear Soldiers, Hello fellows!

I don't know if you have ever heard of Hopkins, but maybe you can place it if I tell you we live between Minneapolis and Lake Minnetonka (a few miles from the lake). We are just getting some spring weather here, the trees are beginning to bud and the birds are coming north again. Perhaps you would like to know more about me. First of all, I am not a blonde! I am 21, tall and slender with brown hair and eyes. My hobbies are sports, music and radio. That's enough about these parts. I hope you will tell me all about yourself and what you like to do in your leisure time.

Sincerely, Miss Gloria Shulstad, Hopkins, Minnesota.

Mom told me that more than 550 letters arrived at Camp Claiborne, and they were spread out on a table. Each of the soldiers chose one. My dad and his bunkmate drew envelopes and when my dad saw the return address on his roomie's envelope—Hopkins, Minnesota, he asked for a trade.

May 18, 1941
Dear Miss Shulstad,
We were given your letters last week, and I traded with my bunkmate for your letter when I saw the return address. My home is Wayzata, Minnesota which is quite a friendly rival with Hopkins, isn't it? Do you know Wayne Wilcox, I think he lives in Hopkins.

This Army life is quite a change, but I like it OK. As for a description of myself: I am 25 years old, 5'11" tall and weigh 175 pounds. Hunting and fishing are my special likes. As for leisure, we have very little, it is even hard to get letters written. Hoping that this small note gives you some idea of things in the sunny south.
Sincerely, Robert Brownton.

May 28, 1941
Dear Robert,
I hope you don't mind me greeting you by your first name. I think first names are much more friendly. Please do call me Gloria.

I received your letter and was surprised to hear from someone from Wayzata whom I never knew. I know quite a few people from Wayzata. I do not know Wayne Wilcox. Bye for now, Pvt. or Mr.?
Sincerely, Gloria Shulstad.

A next letter did not come—June, July. Mom told me that she waited and wondered. She started numerous letters, but decided not to send them until she heard again from Robert. Her mind went from disappointment to worry to irritation. But summer was in full swing and she had plenty of free time even with her second shift job in the ordinance plant. She spent some of her time at Shady Oak beach, meeting up with girlfriends. There were not too many young men around during the war. But mostly, she and her friends were called on to help with odd jobs at home and around the neighborhood. They delivered groceries on Saturdays when the rationed food supplies came in to grocery store, they took a morning shift at the city works, where they assisted with the city victory garden, and helped out wherever needed.

Then finally, on the 28th of August a letter appeared in her mailbox. She was almost afraid to open it.

August 3, 1941
Dear Gloria,
I'm sorry not to have given your last letter a quicker response, but after coming in from training every day a person doesn't feel like writing. But I think of you almost every day.
Sincerely, Robert

Whew! What a relief. The letters started to come more regularly—usually every week or two.

December 14, 1941
Dear Gloria,
Things can certainly change in a few days' time, can't they? The declaration of war has cleared up a lot of things. Training will be speeded up and all furloughs have been canceled.
Sincerely, Robert

January 25, 1942
Dear Gloria,
I know this will be quite a surprise to you. We are on the water going to ? We cannot disclose where we will be, but our mailing address is through the Postmaster at New York by V-mail. We have been sailing about four days now and most of us boys have cases of seasickness. Thanks for the swell letter and the snapshot. By the way, you have never told me your birthday. I will write when I can.
Yours sincerely, Robert.

I asked my mom, "What is V-mail?"

She told me that it stood for "Victory Mail," and V-mail was a valuable tool for the military during World War Two. The military took all correspondence and put it onto a microfilm for shipping. She said, "This saved valuable cargo space for war materials. When the microfilm arrived in the U.S., it was blown up and delivered. V-mail was our best communication tool. When I heard that, I was a big fan. We were all eager for the war to end successfully."

Mom was tired, and so I took the letters home and continued to read.

March 3, 1942
Dear Robert,
I received your V-mail dated January 24 just yesterday, and I was so glad to hear from you. I am glad you liked the snapshot. I wish you could have come through Minneapolis on your way to New York, I can't wait to meet you. About my birthday. I won't be another year older until around Thanksgiving. To be exact, November 25. Keep that spirit, Yours, Gloria.

North Ireland
November 15, 1942
Dearest Gloria,
Mail has been very slow . . .
I hope this reaches you before your birthday.
Love, Bob

December 9, 1942
Dearest Bobby,
I have been thinking about you so much. I got the cable yesterday and I was so thrilled to get it, Bob. It was thoughtful and sweet of you to send birthday wishes. I am grateful to get every letter and card.
Loads of love for always, Yours, Gloria.

V-Mail Courtship

As I read through letter after letter, so carefully organized and dated, it began to sink in. The letters I had read so far spanned a year and a half, and I was only a quarter of the way through them. In a year and a half of once a week letters, my mom and dad had formed an endearment and a history without ever meeting face to face.

Somewhere in North Africa
January 17, 1943
Dearest Gloria,
I got your letter of December 9, just after landing here. It is wonderful that so many of our letters are getting through. This is a great fruit country with lots of oranges, tangerines, almonds and olives.
Yours, Bob

2 Years . . .

July 18, 1943
Dearest Gloria,
Being overseas so long, lots of the boys have been "dropped" by their girls back home. It's really tough to take. We'll both be faithful won't we, dear?
Love, Bob

August 3, 1943
Dearest Bobby,
Hi, sweetheart. I'm still waiting for you and we'll pray it won't be too long now, darling.
Love, Gloria

December 22, 1943
To Gloria,
We join Robert in greetings and wishes for a blessed Christmas.
Cordially, Mr. & Mrs. Brownton

3 Years . . .

    July 30, 1944
    Dearest Bobby,
    Another week, another letter to you, honey. Do you know that we have corresponded for over three years now, about every week. That's a bunch of mail, isn't it? Be thinking of you always.
    Yours, with love, Gloria

    Northern Italy
    January 10, 1945
    My dearest Gloria,
    Your good letters have been coming thru fine. We've really got a lot of snow now and real winter. I notice some of the natives are using skis, and they really go fast on these hills.
    With love, Bob.

4 Years . . .

    May 27, 1945
    My dearest Bob,
    I was glad to get your May 15 V-mail, dear, but I had hoped you would be starting to come home. Certainly, as long as you were ready for a furlough you should be allowed to come now. It's hard at times to understand the breaks. You are so right when you say it has been an awfully long time. Well, honey, we'll just keep pitching 'til we win out. I'm so anxious to see you, dear.
    Lovingly yours, Gloria

And then . . .

    June 25, 1945— Western Union
    Miss Gloria Shulstad
    Arrived safely. Expect to see you soon. Don't attempt to contact or write me here.
    Love, Bob.

V-Mail Courtship

I had become so engrossed reading about this "V-Mail Courtship" that endured great distance and time, I wanted the letters to continue. I knew how the story ended, with a wedding at the family homestead in Wayzata and soon a family growing on that same site. My brother and I are evidence of that, but what happened next? What happened when my mom and dad met after a four-and-a-half year V-mail courtship? What was their reaction when they finally met face to face?

I couldn't wait to talk to my mom again. I wanted to know how and when they decided to marry. I wanted to know about how my dad proposed and whether it was love at first sighting.

That part of the story was left untold. There were no more letters, only memories locked in my mom's heart.

Before I could ask the rest of my questions, Mom died peacefully in her sleep—on Christmas Day. My last memory of her is on the handmade four-poster bed that she and dad shared for 61 years, her hands crossed over her heart and a serene smile on her face. I will ponder all of these things in my heart.

Love came down at Christmas as a baby, who wrapped the whole world in the blanket of his love. His mom, Mary, treasured all these things and pondered them in her heart. (Luke 2:19). My mom went home to be with her soldier on Christmas, treasuring all these words in her heart. May you know peace and joy and love, as you treasure and ponder these things in your heart today. Merry Christmas.

Luke 2:15-20

When the angels had left them and gone into heaven, the shepherds said to one another, 'Let us go now to Bethlehem and see this thing that has taken place, which the Lord has made known to us.' So they went with haste and found Mary and Joseph, and the child lying in the manger. When they saw this, they made known what had been told them about this child; and all who heard it were amazed at what the shepherds told them. But Mary treasured all these words and pondered them in her heart. The shepherds returned, glorifying and praising God for all they had heard and seen, as it had been told them.

Yule Sleigh

by S. Lindy Purdy

My name is Joy Holladay and I was born on Christmas Day. I share my birthday with the Prince of Peace, the Light of the world, the babe in a manger. I am the owner of The Yule Sleigh on Evergreen Lane in Pine City, Minnesota (Y-U-L-E S-L-E-I-G-H— not like You'll Slay).

I have always loved Christmas more than any other time of year. I love the music, the decorations, the baby in the manger, the cookies, the whole family-getting-together-thing. I love that there are traditions that transcend generations, even when we can't quite remember why or how they became traditions. Traditions like stockings hung "by the chimney with care." That tradition started with a legend about a recently widowed father of three girls who was having a very difficult time making ends meet. Even though his daughters were beautiful, he worried that their financial situation would make it impossible for them to marry. St. Nicholas was wandering through the town where the man lived, and heard the villagers discussing the family's plight. He wanted to help, but knew the man would refuse any kind of charity. So instead, one night he slid down their chimney with a bag full of gold coins. He found the girls' socks freshly laundered and hanging by the fireplace to dry. He quickly filled each stocking with coins and then he disappeared.

Traditions are so important at Christmas time. I'm sure each one of you could share a tradition that you have. One of the traditions in our family is "the last ornament standing." We all gather to "undecorate" the tree, and the race is to see who can take the last ornament off the tree. Sometimes it is only found after we drag the tree behind the car, down to the collection area at the park. I love traditions.

Another thing you might want to know is that I am a CGC—a Certified Gift Consultant. I love finding just the right gift for every occasion and for every person on my Christmas list. I even help my friends. It is like a puzzle or a quest to decipher and discover the perfect gift that will delight even the most difficult to please. In fact, my gift selecting abilities led me into this chapter of my story.

And maybe the last thing that is important to know, is that I have three wonderful younger sisters, and six nieces and nephews. Once upon a time, I dreamed and prayed for a child of my own, but God gave me three beautiful neices and three amazing nephews, and I love them with all my heart. Finding the right gifts for each of them has been motivation and inspiration for me.

Back to the story. 2006 was a turning point for me. My career with Nordic Ware in Research and Development had taken me all over the world. I had a condo in downtown Minneapolis in the warehouse district, and I enjoyed my travels and my time at home. I was the first child, eager to spread my wings, and I could not resist the lure of the big city of Minneapolis.

But my best times were when I could be with family, and witness the ever-changing lives of my nieces and nephews: Harrison always busy with school and sports, Henry game for any opportunity to explore parks and museums, Bella singing solos in the Cherub Choir at church, Joey with scouting and tennis, Jenna interested in anything that required a ball to kick, throw, shoot or hit and baby Jordie, she just watched with wonder—trying to do everything the big kids did.

Sundays were family days, and I looked forward to them more and more. All of my sisters and their families lived near Duluth where we all grew up, and where my parents still live. So, every Sunday I got up early and drove up Highway 35 to spend the day with family—two hours and nine minutes door to door. I loved my life, but more and more I found myself wondering what was next.

About that time, my neighbor Carol, who was a sales rep for UMAGA Gift Mart, invited me to attend the Annual Christmas Gift Show. When I walked in to the huge warehouse, it was pure magic. I saw rows and rows of Christmas trees and twinkling lights everywhere. There were displays of candles and creches, toys and books, glass balls and stuffed ornaments, stars and angels. It was like I was in a snow globe of wonder, with Christmas as far as the eye could see.

Yule Sleigh

These ARE a few of "My Favorite Things"
Red and green ribbons on packages tied up,
Candles and cookies and fir trees that light up,
Snow covered chimneys, and festive hung stockings
These are a few of my favorite things.

Santas and angels, and sparkling snowflakes
Sleigh bells and church bells and fresh fruity rum cakes
Babe in a manger and three fancy kings
These are a few of my favorite things,

When the snow flies, when the choir sings
Christmastime is near,
And so I remember my favorite things,
And then it is time to cheer!

Wow! I can still remember that day. I knew in that moment, that my future would have something to do with Christmas. I wanted it to be Christmas all year long, I wanted to somehow make wishes come true and help others find the magic and spirit of Christmas. Not just the glitzy, gifty Christmas spirit, but the true gift of Christmas in the midst of the wrapping paper and decorations, the parties and pageants. I could hardly wait till the next day when I would be with my family and share my new found calling. I knew they would be excited!

Early on Sunday, I started for the family home. I knew the road so well, I scarcely noticed the landscape slip by. I was so deep in thought and dreams of the next chapter of my life, that before I knew it, I looked up and saw the familiar exit for Pine City. It was a "sign," I am sure. So, I took that exit, not knowing exactly why, and found myself on the strip with all the fast food restaurants and gas stations. I decided to make this unplanned detour at least useful, so I pulled into the Quik Stop to get gas.

Next to the gas station was a small shop with photos in the window of available real estate in Pine City—cabins, gift shops, even a strip mall. My eye was immediately drawn to a log cabin, set in a grove of pine trees. I had to see this place. Amazingly, there was a woman in the realty shop on a Sunday morning (another sign) and she gave me the information I wanted. I drove through the town and about two miles north on Hwy. 61 to Evergreen Lane. There it was—embedded in a grove of pine trees. It exuded Christmas. I could see myself, the Certified Gift Consultant, with a Christmas shop that sold and shipped "just the right" gifts all over the world.

An hour later, armed with brochures and a phone full of photos, I proceeded to Duluth. The miles sped by, and I was ready to burst with excitement as I entered the door of my parents' home. Bella and Henry and Jenna were there to greet me at the door, and soon I was exploding with the good news of this new life opportunity—a year-round Christmas Shoppe in Pine City, Minnesota.

THE ROOM WENT SILENT. Mouths hung open with expressions of disbelief. My sister said, "You're kidding, aren't you?" Stan piped in, "Pine City? Didn't we used to play them in sectionals?" "Christmas as a career?"

It was obvious that I needed to do a better job of selling them on this BIG idea. They thought I was crazy, and they acted disappointed. What happened to the cool aunt with the big city condo and the world-traveling job—PINE CITY?

But Dad promised to go with me that next week and scout it out, and since no one could get me to come off cloud-nine, we celebrated and dreamed about this new possibility.

The next months were a whirlwind. By June 3rd, I was the proud owner of a log cabin in the Pine City forest only one hour south of Duluth, and there was work to be done. I enlisted the whole family for clean-up and restoration. I met with the Pine County Building Inspector, a guy named Bud, who grew up in Pine City. Our first meeting was a bit rough, he had a stack of regulations that seemed insurmountable. But he also provided the name of a guy who could make it all happen. I'm not saying it was easy, but somehow we got through it.

After meeting with Bud off and on during the summer, we got to know each other pretty well. He took a real interest in my new project, and even came up with the name, "Yule Sleigh." Catchy—don't you think? Just right for a place full of cool Yule gifts that could be delivered to friends and loved ones—the nice ones, not the naughty ones.

I started modestly with a dozen different themed gift baskets, some Nordic Ware baking items complete with recipes, and a line of hypo-allergenic stuffed animals with ID collars. Each purchase included postage and shipping. With Bud's help and a little computer knowledge, we were able to get the word out, and the doors opened October 25th, 2006.

Over the next years, with a few live reindeer (Dancer and Prancer), lots of hot cider and local musicians, the concept caught on. Yule Sleigh became a destination for Christmas shoppers year-round. We added ornaments, trees, candles and lights, puzzles and games, a full line of Christmas music, and many unique gifts—all with a personalized touch.

It was becoming so important to me that we find gifts for all children, so we installed a North Pole collection area for donated gifts that would go to needy families. That little corner of the shop was heaped high with toys that were distributed through the County Food Bank.

But the real growth came three years ago when we hit upon the idea of delivering each gift in a unique package designed to look like a sleigh, hand-stamped with the return address of the North Pole. This took some cooperation from the US Postal Service—and our wonderful carrier, Barb. As the sleigh-box was opened, a personal message from Santa greeted the recipient. Brilliant!

A year later, we began shipping layettes to an orphanage in Haiti, in a box designed to look like a manger with a star above it. The recorded message of children singing "Jesus Loves Me" played when the package was opened. The layettes were donated and funded through the generosity and gratitude of our customers. So far, we have shipped 317 and we should hit 500 this year.

Things were going well, my nieces and nephews were growing fast and I tried hard to keep up with their ever expanding activities. Then two years ago, Earl walked into the story. Earl is Bud's older brother. He left Pine City for college, then law school at the University of Minnesota before beginning a career in the legal department of an ad agency in Chicago. He was amazingly handsome and a bit flashy for Pine City, but everyone knew him and greeted him with the affection due a hometown son.

It was hard not to notice that the whole town seemed a little different with Earl around. We formally met on the second night of his homecoming, when Bud brought him to visit the Yule Sleigh. I'm not sure why I cared about his reaction, but I did. He was quite something, I must admit. In fact, he took my breath away. I babbled on for a while about reindeer and camels and angels and Santa, totally messing up the images of Christmas. It was easy to be confused when Earl was staring at me. I would be glad when he left to go back to his big-city job and his big-city life.

He seemed duly impressed with Yule Sleigh, and he noticed even the smallest touches. As he left, he asked if I would meet him for dinner the following night. It sounded like a date.

I learned the next morning from Bud, that Earl had been married briefly, and that his wife left him a month after the wedding. She left without an explanation—and Earl was heart-broken. The annulment went through quickly, and he took a leave of absence from his job to backpack through South America before landing here in Pine City.

We did have dinner the next night, and the night after and most nights after that. A few months later, Earl opened a law office on Main Street in Pine City and decided to stay. Our courtship was kind of fast. For me, I knew immediately that I had finally found the love of my life, and I guess Earl felt the same way. We were married that Christmas Eve, and the whole town turned out to celebrate with us. Our families were delighted. Now that's the perfect Christmas gift.

What happened last Christmas is what I really came here to tell you. Earl and I went to the Children's Christmas Pageant at All Saint's Community Church. This is an annual event for my family. Four of my six nieces and nephews were in the cast. Henry was playing the role of the Angel Gabriel. Secretly, he has always held a special place in my heart, he is truly an angel.

We got there early enough to get good seats, and watch as the parents crowded in and the kids nudged and squirmed. The excitement was growing, as the shepherds were waiting off stage right, staffs flying; Kings stage left, crowns askew; and angels wing-to-wing hovering nervously. All the stable animals were in their parents' laps, just waiting. My stomach was in my throat. The pageant always hits me so hard. Just seeing little children heightens my sense of joy and longing. Just as the pageant began, Earl squeezed my hand, knowing just the right thing to do.

As the shepherds and their flocks appeared on stage, the Angel Gabriel stepped onto the top of a riser and pronounced,

"Do not be afraid, for I bring you Good News Joy, for to you a child is given."

Wait a minute—were my ears playing tricks on me—what did I just hear? Did Henry say, *"Do not be afraid, I bring you Good News Joy,* something about a child??" I had prayed it so often, even knowing that it was not medically possible for me. A child? Get a grip. I can still feel my heart race and my face flush when I think about that moment. How crazy—but I know the Bible says, with God all things are possible—but a child?

I felt like Sarah or Elizabeth—much too old to have a child, it really wasn't possible. The rest of the pageant sped by as I sat both treasuring and denying what my ears thought they heard.

Afterwards, Earl and I were back home sipping hot chocolate and thinking about the busy season ahead. The pageant that day had really touched my heart—and the ache would not go away. Earl and I had talked about adopting a child, but it never seemed to be the right time to do it. I tried to block those angel words out of my memory—but they echoed through me—unbidden. The babe of Bethlehem was such a remarkable gift—but that year he brought an ache of longing for me.

The next morning we were up bright and early, ready for the busiest weeks of our year. We were still receiving inventory and running out of room to store it. The hot items for us last year were the Stuffed Safari Animals with a game blanket, and the Burrito Basket, complete with ceramic cooking stone. We also re-ordered stock of "The Game of Me" three different times.

Before we even opened our doors to customers that morning, the bell rang and Earl answered it. All I could hear was, "Joy come quickly." There in the entry was a beautiful woman with a child in her arms. I couldn't take my eyes off the baby, what a beautiful child. We found out that the little girl's name was Sophia, and the woman with her was Elizabeth. Earl suggested we all sit, for Elizabeth had quite a story to tell.

Elizabeth began by telling Earl that Sophia was his daughter. After that I don't think I heard anything clearly. How could that be? Who was her mother? Why didn't he tell me he was a father? Questions were ringing in my head.

As the story unfolded, we learned that Sophia was conceived during Earl's marriage to Lucy. But she left Earl quietly before her pregnancy was discovered. She loved Earl with all her heart, but she had kept a secret from him that she couldn't live with. She had a rare form of dystonia, for which there is no cure. She couldn't face burdening Earl with this devastating news, so she fled to her Aunt Elizabeth's home where she would live out her days.

Sophia was a total surprise. Lucy survived the pregnancy, but the effort of childbirth had taken a terrible toll on her. She went into a coma a month later. Under duress, Elizabeth promised Lucy that she would not contact Earl until she was gone. She died October 20th, but it took Elizabeth almost two months to trace Earl's movements from U of M Law School, to Leo Burnett in Chicago, to South America and to the little town of Pine City, Minnesota.

But here she was just two weeks before Christmas, with Earl's child in her arms. Sophia. "Would we?" "Could we?" My heart ached for this child, and my head was twirling. Earl looked at me and said, "Joy, can we?"

"YES, YES, a thousand times YES." Sophia was the most perfect gift I could have imagined. My hands trembled and I thought my heart would burst with joy. I held Sophia and Earl held us both. A baby, a family, a miraculous gift from God.

Somehow God spoke to me on that December day through the words of the Angel Gabriel, preparing my heart for a child. And I know that God speaks to each of us, urging us to prepare our hearts for Jesus, to get ready for Immanuel, God with us—our most perfect gift.

Luke 2:10-14
The angel said,
"Do not be afraid; for see—I am bringing you good news of great joy for all the people: to you is born this day in the city of David a Savior, who is the Messiah, the Lord.
This will be a sign for you: you will find a child wrapped in bands of cloth and lying in a manger."
And suddenly there was with the angel a multitude of the heavenly host, praising God and saying,
"Glory to God in the highest heaven, and on earth peace among those whom he favors!"

Mark 10:27
Jesus said, "For mortals it is impossible, but not for God; for with God all things are possible."

MERRY CHRISTMAS.

NORTH POLE

by S. Lindy Purdy

My name is Angela, Angela Jingle and I just graduated in May from the Colorado School of Mines in Golden, Colorado, with a degree in metallurgy and water ecology.

I have an amazing story to tell you about "reindeer" and "stars" and "sleighs." But before I get into the story, it is important for you to know that I have always been interested in environmental issues and I love science of any kind. As a kid I collected everything—rocks, butterflies, leaves, flowers, bones, even sand from different beaches. My dad dedicated one whole side of our garage for my collections and specimens. There are shelves from floor to ceiling, and every shelf holds some important treasure.

But the other obsession that I have had since as long as I can remember is with the North Pole—both the mythical one (which is real by the way) and the geographic one (which is not really a particular place, but in reality is two places—the magnetic north pole and the true North Pole.) And to be quite honest with you, I am very worried about both right now.

My interest in The North Pole (Santa's domain) began when I was four. I wrote letters every December to Santa Claus, at 365 Nicholas Street, Claustown, North Pole. Did you know that The North Pole even has its own ZIP Code, HOHOHO, assigned by the Canadian government? On a side note, Canada claims the North Pole, as does Alaska, Finland, Norway and Russia.

Anyway, for many years I wrote to Santa, and every year I got a beautiful card back, with a great photo of Mr. Claus himself, with his lovely wife, Mrs. It was postmarked from Claustown, North Pole, HOHOHO, and the message always had a great impact on me. "You better watch out, you better not cry, you better not pout I'm telling you why, Santa Claus is coming to town." In the return letter there was always a little bit of magic dust that looked just like baking powder. I actually saved all that magic dust in a jar that I kept on a bookshelf in my bedroom.

Over the years, I moved from writing letters asking for gifts for myself, to asking for special gifts for others. I was truly amazed when I found out that Santa actually responded to those requests.

One year, my friend Sally's house burned down the day after Thanksgiving. Her family went to live with relatives while the house was being rebuilt. The one thing she missed most was her Hugga-Bugga bear that she originally got from Santa. It was not just the regular Hugga-Bugga bear, it was the one with the soft pink polka dots. Hugga-Bugga Pink Polka Dot Bear was not something that was easily replaced. In my letter that year, I asked Santa to search all his warehouses and make sure that Sally got that special, particular bear. Good old Santa came through. Another time I wrote to Santa asking for a baby sister for my friend Emily, and sure enough, she got a baby the next summer, but it was a brother. I think she was quite disappointed for a while, but it all worked out well.

A few years later, I learned that sweet Maggie Green, the post-mistress in my small town of Tower, Minnesota, was sending back return messages from The North Pole to all the kids in town. But I still did not understand how this mysterious process worked. How was it that just the right gifts were being delivered to just the right kids? Maggie must have been one of Santa's helpers, since she had easy access to the postal system. The North Pole was so real to me.

My interest in the geographic North Pole started with a class I took last year about the ecology of the polar ice caps. It was an amazing synergy of my two majors, and the professor, Dr. Olivia Ice, was the most inspiring woman I had ever met. She was a Professor in Residence at the Colorado School of Mines from Lappeenranta University of Technology in Lappeenranta, Finland. Yes, that is a real school and a real place. Dr. Ice and I shared the same passions for the Arctic environment and for Santa (St. Nicholas) and his elves.

In high school, Dr. Ice had been a foreign exchange student in Canada where she became fluent in English. She completed her doctorate at the University of Helsinki in Arctic

Ecology. I am so fortunate that she came to the School of Mines when she did.

Last fall, Dr. Ice invited her students to her home for a Finnish dinner. After dinner, we watched a video of the explorations that are being done in Northern Finland and on Ellesmere Island in the far north of Canada. She was excited to tell us that in January she would be part of a research team traveling in Ellesmere Island to interview the native peoples, the Inuits, and to measure the snow and ice depths around the Inuit village of Grise Fiord. She had never been there before, but had done similar research in the far north of Finland and Norway. She explained to us that she had great fear that the consistently warming temperatures in the last century have been harmful to the delicate balance of wildlife and vegetation in the arctic region. I sure could agree with that.

The last section of the video was a scene from a little village, complete with a workshop, parka clad workers, a sleigh, and even a paddock of reindeer. It was the Santa's workshop of my imagination. My eyes nearly popped out. The sign on the road said, "Grise Fiord, Ellesmere Island, Canada."

A week after that enchanted evening, Dr. Ice announced that she was looking for a student to accompany her to Ellesmere Island in January. I could hardly believe my ears. I lingered after class, and then quickly blurted out, "That would be my dream come true!" She seemed glad to see my excitement, and handed me an application. I raced back to my dorm and read it immediately. This would not be an all-expense-paid trip, and I would have to submit an essay on my professional goals for global environmental education. Ah, finally I knew what to tell my family and friends I am striving for—Global Environmental Education. And my real life world experience might just begin at the North Pole.

My mind was flying. I knew absolutely that I was called to be a teacher—a teacher who could bring curiosity, imagination and a love for our beautiful and fragile world to my students. Now I needed to get my fingers flying on the application form.

Two days and seven edits later, I stood in front of Professor Ice's desk with application in hand. Then the waiting began. One week, two weeks, a month went by. I finally had the courage to tell my mom and dad. They were at once excited for me, and yet worried about how we would pay for this adventure. After all, the cost was more than they could handle. They wished me luck, but told me not to sign anything till final costs were determined.

Then on Friday, just before Thanksgiving break, a letter arrived in my P.O. Box. They chose me! I was going to the North Pole! My dream was coming true—all I needed now was the funds to pay for it.

My parents' next door neighbor, Nancy Barnes, is a reporter for our hometown newspaper, *The Tower News*, and when she heard that I was chosen to go to the North Pole, she wrote about it in her column. When I arrived home for Thanksgiving, everyone in town seemed to know. My friends and relatives rallied behind me with gifts large and small to help finance this once-in-a-lifetime opportunity. I went back to Colorado to finish the semester knowing this dream was going to come true.

At Christmas time, I was treated like the hometown hero, and waiting for me was a packet of tickets, itinerary, and bag tags.

January 1	Minneapolis to Ottawa, Canada
January 3	Arrive Grise Fiord, Ellesmere Island via The Matterhorn
February 4	Private flight to Reykjavik, Iceland
February 5	Reykjavik, Iceland to Minneapolis, Minnesota

This was more than I could quite take in. It was a stunning and glorious Christmas. This gift was way more than anyone could ask for from Santa or anyone else. On Christmas Eve, we all went to church—and when I say all, it really seemed like all of Tower showed up. The church was decorated with twinkling lights, greens, poinsettias, and the traditional crèche that has been on the chancel since before I was born. Pastor Trish read the story of the wise men from the East bringing gifts to the baby Jesus.

As I sat there letting the words sink in, it finally all made sense to me in a tangible way. I could feel it. God is the great gift-giver. God gave us everything, this good creation that we are to care for, the gift of each other to share it and best of all, the gift of God's intimate love incarnate. That is what we celebrate at Christmas. Joy to the world, the

Lord has come. I felt loved by God and by my hometown, as everyone wished me "Merry Christmas and Bon Voyage".

We all found our way home that holy night, but I knew I had found so much more. Somehow, I also knew that I had been given the gift of a lifetime in order to give the gift of my lifetime.

January came in a flash, but not without some fear and trembling. I had never been anywhere that wasn't in Minnesota or Colorado or somewhere in between. I was going to a place where the internet had not yet taken over.

So, let your imagination loose as I take you along with me.

On January 1st, I got off an airplane in Ottawa, and caught a shuttle to the harbor. There I boarded an "ice breaker" ship named The Matterhorn. It had a huge V-shaped prow and a flat deck with a dozen cabins on top, and it was my transportation to Ellesmere Island. The voyage would take two days and this would be the last trip for The Matterhorn until spring. The dark, freezing weather thickened the polar ice cap making it impenetrable for the next four months. I would go home by a different way.

During the two day voyage, the daylight disappeared and we traveled by starlight. I have never seen so many stars. My arrival in the tiny town of Grise Fiord at the top of the world was spectacular. We entered through an ice fjord, illuminated by a dozen flood lights, and pulled up alongside a long pier that went right into the center of town.

At the top of the world, there is only one sunrise, and one sunset every year, so for half of the year it is perpetual night, and for the other half it is day. Through the darkness I could see the lights of Grise Fiord, but I had no idea what time of day or night it was. I was not prepared for what I would find in that magical place.

There were a dozen people waiting to meet the five passengers and the much anticipated cargo. I was met by the other expedition members and was glad to see Dr. Ice among them.

Over the coming days, our research team got to know each other as we worked together and lived life together in an old Army barracks. Dr. Ice assigned teams to work on individual projects, so that we could get the most done in our month in Grise Fiord. My partner turned out to be Dr. Ice's younger brother, Johann Kjerstad, who worked with the Inuit Circumpolar Council (ICC).

Johann and I met with the local Inuit people, a gentle indigenous people who live much as they did thousands of years ago. They welcomed us into their community and shared with us their concerns for their environment, where only a few animals and plants survive. I learned that the Inuits believe that every living thing has a spirit which lives on in the afterlife and we humans have the responsibility to care for every one.

The work we were all doing was rewarding and also discouraging, as we found measurable changes in air, water, and ice that had occurred over the last decade. We were all concerned for these beautiful people, this beautiful place, and for the whole earth.

On our tenth night among the Inuit people a baby was born. The mother was very young, and a little frightened, but her young husband was very loving and encouraging. As the older women helped with the birth, we were invited to sit with the father and other friends to pray and sing. In just three days the baby boy, Ujarak, meaning "the rock", was out and about among us, riding in the hood of his mother's parka. We all adored him, but no one as much as his young parents.

Each night our team would gather and discuss our day and our findings. A deep affection and friendship developed among us as we cared for each other and the earth. I was becoming especially fond of Johann. I admired him so much for the work he was doing and his gentle way with the Inuit people.

Some evenings we would sit around a fire with the Inuit people as they told us their stories and myths. On the very last night before we left they invited us into their big igloo—big enough for about 60 people—for a drum dance. They danced for us to the beautiful music of their drums made of walrus stomachs. By using the stomach of an animal they honor it after its death. Johann sat with me and held my mitten in his hands as we shared this last night with our new friends.

Saying goodbye to Johann, as he left for Finland, was difficult, but he promised to visit me in Tower this summer. And who knows where this trip of a lifetime will lead us? Now that I have graduated, I have applied for a job doing research in the Arctic, so I may just run into him there.

I could tell you that the work was the important part of the trip and hopefully it will make a difference. I could tell you that the most important thing I learned is that there is a place called the North Pole where dreams are captured—both real and imaginary. I could tell you that the most important thing that happened on this trip was earning the trust of the Inuit people. It might have been their invitation to share in the celebration of new life when a child was born in the village, for that was a Holy moment. I could tell you that the most important part of this expedition was gazing up at the deep darkness, filled with a multitude of stars and standing in awe of the vastness of God's good creation.

And all of that would be true. What I know for sure is that we are created and loved, we have been given many good gifts and we are each intended as a gift to each other. God's goodness and love are vast and unknowable—except perhaps through the birth of a baby, the gift of love.

My hope for each of you this Christmas is that you might experience wonder and awe as you celebrate God's good creation and experience anew the gift of love, born to us in Jesus.

Merry Christmas.

The Magi Visit the Messiah
Matthew 2:2-12

After Jesus was born in Bethlehem in Judea, during the time of King Herod, Magi from the east came to Jerusalem and asked, "Where is the one who has been born king of the Jews? We saw his star when it rose and have come to worship him."

When King Herod heard this he was disturbed, and all Jerusalem with him. When he had called together all the people's chief priests and teachers of the law, he asked them where the Messiah was to be born. "In Bethlehem in Judea," they replied, "for this is what the prophet has written:

> *'But you, Bethlehem, in the land of Judah,*
> *are by no means least among the rulers of Judah;*
> *for out of you will come a ruler*
> *who will shepherd my people Israel.' "*

Then Herod called the Magi secretly and found out from them the exact time the star had appeared. He sent them to Bethlehem and said, "Go and search carefully for the child. As soon as you find him, report to me, so that I too may go and worship him."

After they had heard the king, they went on their way, and the star they had seen when it rose went ahead of them until it stopped over the place where the child was. When they saw the star, they were overjoyed. On coming to the house, they saw the child with his mother Mary, and they bowed down and worshiped him. Then they opened their treasures and presented him with gifts of gold, frankincense and myrrh. And having been warned in a dream not to go back to Herod, they returned to their country by another route.